The Magic of THE MEKONG

The Magic of

THE MEKONG

Text and Photographs by
Julie Sarasin

HAWK'S-EYE PUBLICATIONS

Contents

Half title page: *Cargo boat on the Mekong, viewed from the Pak Ou caves, Laos.*
Title page: *Fisherman throwing his net, Khone Falls, Laos.*
Following spreads: *At Nong Khai, Thailand, sunset on the Mekong. At Khong Chiam, Thailand, the cove in the foreground offers ideal mooring.*
Contents page: *Just upriver from Khong Chiam, fishermen drawing their catch.*
This page: *Houseboat moored on the Mekong at Chiang Saen, Thailand.*

Published by Hawk's-Eye Publications Limited Partnership
P.O. Box 1030, Silom Post Office, Bangkok 10504, Thailand
Tel: (66-1) 192-0798

© 2001 photographs and text by Julie Sarasin

© 2001 maps by Hawk's-Eye Publications Limited Partnership

ISBN 974-87800-0-7

Editor: Keith Hardy

Design: Annie Miniscloux, Format & Partners Ltd, Bangkok

Photographic equipment: Pentax ME, Pentax K1000, Pentax ESPIO 105WR

Reproduction: One Hundred Co., Ltd

Printed and bound in Thailand by Sirivatana Interprint Public Co., Ltd

The publisher would like to thank the Tourism Authority of Thailand, whose generous sponsorship has made publication of this book possible.

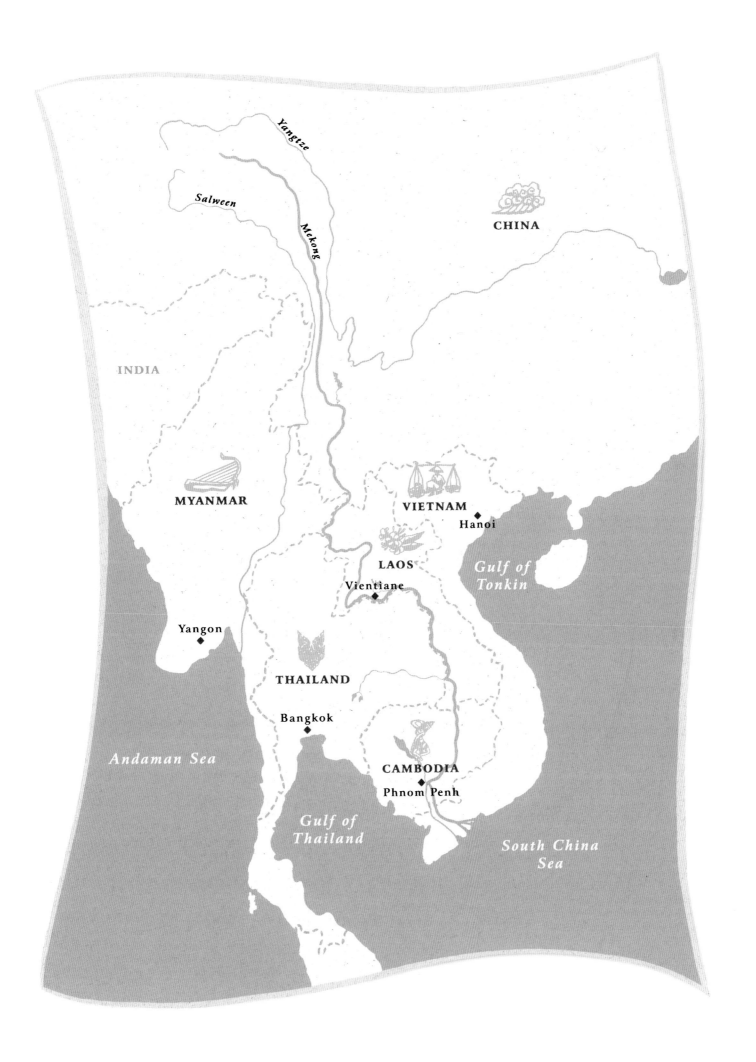

Introduction

There is a profound if apparently contradictory belief that explorers travel and travellers explore. The former remain few in number, whilst the latter are growing apace. As one of the majority, my aim was simply to start from as far up the Mekong River as any serious yet modest traveller might begin, and to travel downriver, stopping to visit river towns and villages, and taking time to explore the hinterland too.

I did not intend to spend all my time on boats but planned to use the river as a sort of mobile base from where I could venture into the interior, away from the river, sometimes doubling back, sometimes swinging round in a loop, sometimes leaving the river and joining it again at the same point, sometimes rejoining downriver and sometimes, of course, travelling down the river itself. I figured that this mix would prove the best way to go, a way to combine both the similar and the varied aspects of life on the river, life by the river, and life away yet never too far from the river.

What follows is a record of what I found, what I experienced, what I learnt, what I saw, what I heard, what I wrote, what I captured on film, what I remember now and what I shall continue to recall in years to come.

The River Mekong flows 4,800 kilometres from source to sea. At 5,000 metres above sea level, on the eastern edge of the Plateau of Tibet, it begins humbly in Qinghai province as a trickle of streams, which merge and transform wondrously into the magnificent, magical Mekong River.

Above: Dai woman polishing rice at her mother's house, Ganlanba, China.
Opposite: Rice terraces, a common sight along the banks of the Mekong.

Above: Monk pointing to a stone inscription at Keng-Zan monastery in Kyaingtong, Myanmar. Above right: Around two dozen fine images of the Buddha reside within the beautiful temple of Wat Jong Kham in Kyaingtong. Opposite: At day's end a young boy poles his bamboo raft towards the edge of Naung Tung lake in Kyaingtong.

From its source, the Mekong passes through or skirts six countries until it reaches journey's end — the South China Sea. Just over half of its entire voyage is through China, where it is first known as Dza Chou, or Water of Stone, soon after becoming known as the Lancang Jiang, or Turbulent River, a name it retains until reaching Laos.

Flowing south from Qinghai, through the autonomous region of Tibet, the Lancang Jiang continues through some of the most spectacular landscapes of Yunnan, a province fondly known as 'South of the Clouds'. Yunnan is the fourth-largest province in China, is populated by around 37 million people and contains 24 separate ethnic groups. Almost half of all China's ethnic groups inhabit this province, which makes it a fascinating place to witness an amazing tapestry of cultural identities, deeply entrenched despite the omnipresent national influence.

The river then forms the natural border between China and Myanmar until, shortly after, China gives way to Laos. Now the Mekong follows a southwesterly course between Myanmar and Laos, serving as direct two-way access between the two countries.

Then, at the heart of the Golden Triangle, there is three-way access where the Thai border joins both the Myanmar and Lao borders, though the three borders adjoin only at the confluence point of the Ruak and Mekong rivers. Thus the Mekong bears witness to much cross-border migration, cultural exchange and trade. Then, swinging southeastwards, the Mekong becomes the border between Laos and Thailand where, in both countries, it is known by its local name of the Mae Nam Khong.

But soon, the Mekong leaves Thailand behind, striking east through Laos, rounding Luang Prabang, before eventually returning in a generally southern direction to the Thai border again. Laos shares its border with

Above: *Caught near the Khone Falls in southern Laos, this fish weighs in at 25 kilos.*
Above right: *Young Lao Soung woman blending traditional and modern fashion, revealing a direction of today's hilltribe culture.*
Opposite: *Dressed Lanna-style, young man with ceremonial umbrella, during Songkran, Chiang Saen, Thailand.*

China, Myanmar, Vietnam, Thailand and Cambodia, thus making it the only country with the distinction of having a border with all the other countries through which the Mekong flows. With a population of only 4.6 million, Laos is comprised of 47 main ethnic groups and a total of 149 subgroups. Without question, the country is one of the most culturally diverse in Southeast Asia. Along with its neighbours Myanmar and Cambodia, Laos has begun to open up to the outside world after decades of self-imposed isolation.

The Mekong continues to bring great blessings to the people of the northern and northeastern provinces of Thailand. Through generations, the Thai have revered the river for the fertile plains it creates when its waters overflow, for the bountiful supply of fish it provides, and for the vital communication link it offers within the region, especially with neighbouring Laos. Today, it is evident that a wave of development has finally arrived at its banks, not insofar as to spoil it, but in giving more than just a glimmer of hope to this once-neglected region that the relative prosperity of some other parts of present-day Thailand may become accessible to all.

Many would say that the most interesting part of the Mekong is from the Golden Triangle down to the Cambodian border. For along this part of the Mekong, Laos and Thailand see the greatest range of the Mekong's attitudes — narrow defiles, gentle plains, churning rapids and unnavigable falls.

Others, though, would say that the most interesting part is yet to come. In Cambodia, before long the Mekong quietens down to become a typical lowland river, broad, lazy, and with plenty of river traffic. There is no hint yet of the amazing natural phenomenon which lies ahead.

Above: Such excitement! These children on the banks of the Mekong River at Nong Khai, Thailand, are thrilled with their catch.
Above right: Some men fish with nets, others fish with traps. Here, at Khong Chiam in Thailand, it is the end of the day and time to dive down for that last basket, hoping the Mekong has yielded more of its bounty.

Cambodia once was the heart of the great Khmer Empire, between the ninth and fourteenth centuries. And at the heart of that empire was Angkor, close to the Tonle Sap, or Great Lake. When the monsoon rains come, the Mekong's feeder, the Tonle Sap River, achieves the seemingly impossible. It reverses its flow, emptying excess water from the Mekong into the Great Lake, which swells enormously. The net result is an immense food supply, of vital benefit to the majority of Cambodia's 11.5 million people, who live under the direct influence of the Mekong as it traverses the country for 450 kilometres from north to south.

At Phnom Penh, the Mekong divides into two for its passage into the southernmost part of Vietnam. In this final country of its mighty journey, the Mekong River is known locally as the Cuu Long, meaning Nine Dragons, a reference to the river's many mouths. In southern Vietnam, the Mekong creates a most fertile plain, emerald and lush, rich with alluvial soil and silt sediment deposits, which year by year add to the coastline of this country. It is here in the Mekong Delta that one finds the economic heart of an ever-thriving nation. And it is here, also, that the epic journey of the Mekong River reaches its destination as its waters pour into the South China Sea.

For centuries, this prodigious flow of water has touched the lives of generations of river-dwelling and river-dependent peoples. A vital life

force to some 65,000,000 residents of southwestern China, Myanmar, Laos, Thailand, Cambodia and Vietnam, this revered waterway continues to bear silent witness to scenes of celebration and tragedy and, most constant of all, sightings of change.

The majority of the people who inhabit the Mekong valley and its surroundings have been classified by ethnologists as belonging to the Tai–Kadai language group of peoples, most of whom originated from southern China. Today, their descendants still live in well-established, identifiable groupings or tribes, many of whom remain faithful to their traditional lifestyle, customs, language and unique dress inherited from their ancestors.

The rugged nature of the upper reaches of the river, the relative isolation of northwestern Laos, eastern Myanmar and northern Thailand, and the beneficial influence of the Mekong on food supply have been powerful contributory factors in the areas along its banks remaining intact and relatively unspoiled. But the burning question is, for how long? And what will greater accessibility, burgeoning tourism and technological developments bring to this paradise, still predominantly untouched by the modern world?

Above: Tower-shrines, *Banteay Srei temple, Cambodia. Built of pink sandstone, and with fine ornamentation, Banteay Srei, though quite small, is very beautiful.*
Above left: Sold out! Vietnamese women returning from market with their boat emptied of produce.

China

My sense of anticipation was overflowing. Tomorrow would see me arrive at the starting point of my journey down the Mekong River. Journey down the Mekong? Easier said than done.

The problem with travelling down the Mekong is that for the China section of the river such an objective is impossible to achieve. From Tibet down to the south of Yunnan, there are no riverboats to take you. Almost nobody needs or wants to go down a river fraught with almost unrelenting, turbulent danger, a river running through desolate and largely uninhabited terrain. Even though it is indeed possible to travel on the river briefly in some places, what do you do when the river's menace just ahead forces you to disembark from your boat, in the middle of nowhere, no towns, no villages, no roads, no people, no nothing?

But I had to go see for myself. If I could just go to somewhere high up the river, somewhere in northwestern Yunnan, somewhere that was at least reachable, it would suffice for now and I would work my way down through the villages and towns of Yunnan until the river had calmed down and was ready to receive me more hospitably.

And so it was that with one night to go before I reached my initial goal, I found myself in Weixi County in northwestern Yunnan. Here in the dusty, sleepy and rather poor town of the same name, where not much happens and there is little entertainment save guessing how long it

Low water, Mekong River, northwestern Yunnan province. The suspension bridge links a small Bai–Lisu town with the local school.

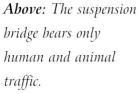

Above: The suspension bridge bears only human and animal traffic.

Above right: Typical village dwelling in northwestern Yunnan, overlooking the Mekong River.

Opposite: Mountain stream, near to the Jiang–Giao hot spring, northwestern Yunnan.

will be before your breath will freeze, the best guesthouse available offered a flask of hot water as a substitute for the running-hot genuine article. Nonetheless, in Weixi this seemed a luxury and thus I was thankful for even such minor comfort.

Anticipating an early night and wondering what inhabitants of Weixi count instead of sheep to fall asleep, I was delighted when my driver, Mr. Hur (suitably named — he drove like a charioteer!), took me to the house of his brother where I became his brother's dinner guest. The house was built on two floors and was larger than most other houses in the area. Once inside, my driver announced to me, with great pride, that his brother held a good job at the local electricity power station and that his sister-in-law also worked nearby. My host's wife kindly treated me to a wonderful home-cooked Naxi meal consisting of ginger-flavoured chicken soup, fried green vegetables, and thinly sliced flour-covered strips of potato fried with sliced onions and spring onions, accompanied by steamed rice. It was absolutely delicious.

The next morning saw us in our Chinese-built Cherokee-style jeep, churning up the dust as we drove towards the Mekong. But the dust we created was mostly behind us and I was able to appreciate the splendid scenery to the full, though not the potholed zigzagging roads.

After two teeth-gritting hours we stopped at a really beautiful stream known as the You-Chun. My guide, Mr. Zhao, told me that it flows into the Lancang Jiang, the name of the Mekong River in Yunnan. He was all excitement as he explained that the stream contains the

famous Jiang–Giao hot spring where Lisu, Naxi and Yi come to take part in their annual water-cleansing celebration. Entirely surrounded by large mountains and rock columns, the site is quite splendid. Certainly it has a special atmosphere and, after having been rather exhausted by the long, arduous journey towards the Mekong, and having felt rather fragile, I now felt rejuvenated just from being at this cool, relaxing place.

Back in the jeep, in just five minutes we came to a river, and not just any river. I found myself looking at a sparkling stretch of water spanned by a packhorse and pedestrian suspension bridge. This was the Lancang Jiang; this was the Mekong River!

On the river at this point were two boats that had seen better days. The water level was low and the scene very peaceful. The two boats, moored close to the bank, had been adapted for the purpose of panning for gold. I was told this was a common sight along the river many years ago but that today there is barely enough of the precious metal in evidence to render such activity worthwhile.

Distracting me from the old boats moored along the river, Mr. Hur took me into the local village to eat. In this part of Yunnan, he has

Above: *Inhabitants of the Bai-Lisu village consider themselves fortunate to be blessed with one of the very few bridges over the Mekong.*

Opposite: *Boats used by local people when panning for gold on the Mekong River in northwestern Yunnan.*

acquired the reputation of knowing just where to find the finest noodles, and served by the prettiest girls, too. The dishes came with spicy chilli sauce that together with the hot soup helped relieve the effects of Yunnan's cold weather.

We were in a small town inhabited by ethnic Bai and Lisu, little more than 100 kilometres south of the border with Tibet. At this point, the Mekong River runs southwards, flanked by two other mighty rivers, the Yangtze to its east and the Salween to the west. Later, the Salween will strike its way into northeastern Myanmar, then skirt the eastern border with Thailand before flowing through southern Myanmar and emptying into the Gulf of Martaban. The Yangtze escorts the Mekong only briefly before a U-turn takes it away on an irregular course through northern Yunnan, Sichuan province and then across central China until it flows into the East China Sea.

Downriver on the Mekong is Gangantang town, nearby which is a village inhabited by migrants from Tibet. Some of the houses in the village are constructed of timber and brick, and their wooden verandahs are put to good purpose for drying corn and radishes, just harvested.

Above: Houses cluster together on the mountain slopes, surrounded by farmland and, beyond, pine trees.
Opposite: Wheeled transport lacks the versatility of ponies in and around the mountain towns close to the Mekong.

Above: Crispy rice and sugar confections, especially popular on festive and other special occasions.

Opposite: Tibetan-style bridge over a small river in the mountains between the Mekong and Yangtze rivers.

Their living area is on the first floor, while their livestock shelter is below at ground level.

This stretch of the river is difficult to travel; there is no suitable river transport and the roads, little more than barely passable dirt tracks, mostly strike inland and do not follow the course of the river. So already, I was to venture inland, for there was little other choice. We drove through isolated villages, occasionally stopping to admire a panoramic landscape. There were Lisu villages, Bai villages, villages of migrants from Tibet, but most of all there were Naxi villages.

Many villages come alive when it is market day and wandering between the stalls can be quite an experience as one sometimes comes across the unexpected. In one Naxi village at which I stopped it seemed as typical as most others — colourful and full of bustle. Row upon row of household items, from batteries and torches to towels and blankets, competed with large, fast-selling soap bars available from the stalls. All the items being offered for sale were made in China. I walked on through the market, my eyes scanning the goods on offer. Suddenly, I stumbled and, looking down, found I had trodden on a pile of dead rats! Before I

could enquire the price of a kilo I learned, to my amazement, that local officials pay other local folk to kill the creatures in an effort to prevent them eating farm produce. The rodents were not for home consumption. Rather, they had been left exposed as proof of their slaughter and a reminder that payment was due.

As the Yangtze flows as little as 50 kilometres from the Mekong in certain parts of Yunnan, I thought I would take a brief look at the world's third-longest river and then work my way southwards between the Yangtze and the Mekong. Early one morning, on my way there, I ran into good fortune for just as I reached Tacheng, a small town not very far from the Yangtze, I saw some kind of celebration taking place not far from the road. Inquisitive, I stopped to see what was happening, learned that it was an ethnic Tibetan wedding celebration, and immediately was invited to join the other guests. All weddings are special and I felt extremely honoured to receive my impromptu invitation. I observed that the men dressed rather plainly in their traditional wear and congregated in an area separate from the women. Indeed, even the wedding banquet was a segregated affair.

Above: As at wedding receptions the world over, the men divide from the women, and this Tibetan community in northwestern Yunnan is no different to anywhere else.

Opposite: Woman at the wedding raising her beautiful skirt a little in genteel fashion as she negotiates some steps.

Women relatives of the bride and groom, and friends, enjoying the wedding feast.

Later that day, I sampled the atmosphere of Tacheng's weekly market. In the event, it was a really lively affair, the streets swarming with people from near and far. Despite muddy, potholed roads, local farmers managed to transport in makeshift barrows a variety of fruit, nuts and vegetables to sell to awaiting womenfolk, while groups of men played board games to while away the time.

That night I stayed in a guesthouse right on the banks of the Yangtze River. Another freezing cold night. Another mercifully hot flask. All night long the sound of rushing river pleasantly disturbed my sleep. In the morning, as planned, I headed south towards Lijiang. Along the way, some of the villages I went through were so small as to be better described as hamlets. These belonged mainly to the Naxi, Bai and Yi, and were surrounded by terraced farms. Apart from their staple diet, rice, they grow only one other regular annual crop, in most cases corn.

Just a short excursion from the road to Lijiang is Shigu, renowned for its strategic location at the 'first bend' of the Yangtze River, where a sixteenth-century Naxi victory over a Tibetan army took place and, in 1936, the point at which the People's Army crossed the river before marching all the way to northern China.

Lijiang is a Naxi town. The Naxi are famed for their written language whereby they use pictographs instead of an alphabet. The town has much to commend it. Greeting the traveller arriving at the old town are charming, pedestrianized, narrow cobbled streets leading to delightful rows of wooden two-storey houses, each possessing a beautiful carved

Above: Heavily laden farmworkers struggling through their village in northwestern Yunnan.
Above left: Yi man with his long-stemmed pipe. He is well-wrapped up to combat the cold air.
Opposite: Yi and Naxi villages amongst the mountains between the Mekong and Yangtze rivers.

After all the activity of harvesting the corn, all is quiet and peaceful at this village by the lake, near Lijiang.

Chain suspension bridge at Shigu. In constant use by local people for over 100 years, its traffic is now reduced due to the recent construction of a nearby concrete bridge.

Above: Women washing clothes and preparing food at the stream in Lijiang.

Opposite: At Meadow Peak, north of Lijiang, Naxi dancers in their traditional costumes, relaxing during an interval in their performance. The snow-capped Yulongxue Shan, or Jade Dragon Snow Mountain, looks down majestically upon them.

door. Rushing through the town is a small, frisky stream that seems to follow you wherever you walk.

Lijiang is blessed with stunning landscape views of the mountains, particularly Yulongxue Shan, or Jade Dragon Snow Mountain. On a clear day it is a spectacular sight, its snow-capped peak glistening in the bright sunlight. I travelled up the mountain by chair lift. At the summit the air was cool and crisp.

Truly sad to leave Lijiang, I moved on southwards again, towards Dali, trying to ignore the discomfort of the bone-rattling roads as we passed through many, many, very poor and rather ramshackle villages. Along the way were orchards with walnut trees, persimmon trees heavy with fruit, and many other trees whose leaves had turned an autumnal shade of gold and russet. They were a welcome distraction from the rough and dusty ride.

The Er Hai Lake lies just east of Dali and channels water into the Mekong by way of the Xi'er River. Elevated at 1,900 metres with a 250-square-kilometre expanse of beautiful bluer-than-blue water and set amidst the mountains, the lake is captivating and exudes a regal presence

*Black Dragon Pool
Park in Lijiang.
In the background,
Yulongxue Shan soars
to over 5,500 metres.*

fit for a king. So it was unsurprising for me to learn that the Bai selected this site, in the eighth century, to establish an independent monarchy, the Nanzhao kingdom, after defeating the Tang imperial army. Two centuries later, a double coup resulted in Nanzhao being superseded by the Dali kingdom. Essentially, the only real difference from the Nanzhao kingdom was a change of king and lineage, the new king's subjects being those inherited, so to speak, from his predecessor. Then, in the thirteenth century, the Dali kingdom fell to the Mongol army of Kublai Khan. During the next century, Yunnan came under the rule of the Ming Dynasty, though its independent nature saw it become more like a colony than a province. In the centuries since, right to this present day, this outpost province of China has

always retained its own distinctive culture, largely because of its strong blend of many ethnic groups.

The Bai have maintained their long-established roots in the Er Hai Lake area, having settled there some 3,000 years ago. The inhabitants of modern-day Dali are still mostly Bai which, translated, means 'white'. Certainly, it is true to say that they are more fair-skinned than most other ethnic Chinese.

I rose while it was still dark, to catch the early morning feel of Dali. In the dim light, just before the sun rose, I watched the silhouette show of people cycling to work, running to catch buses, and the steam from hot dumplings sending aromatic signals that a hot breakfast by the roadside was but a moment away. Calmly, amidst this frenzy of early activity, womenfolk were knitting in front of their shophouses. Although what

Above: Qianxun Pagoda, on a hillside at the edge of Dali. This 16-tiered structure, one of the oldest in south-west China, is 70 metres high.

Above left: Old woman rinsing root vegetables.

Opposite: Old Bai woman selling flowers to diners in a restaurant in Dali.

Sunrise, Er Hai Lake.
Fishermen are about to
come ashore with their
night's catch. In a few
minutes, the fishermen
will go home . . . on
the public bus that
has been waiting
patiently for them!

they knit are usually for their families, one can acquire easily clothing such as knitted slippers in hot primary colours.

Whatever Dali may lack in terms of creature comforts and modern conveniences is outweighed tenfold by the sheer charm of the town and its people. Dali is steeped in history. Most of the old, large houses in the town have high walls, with a courtyard in front of the house, giving the impression that the occupants value their privacy. Bai women have a reputation for trading jewellery, trinkets and decorative embroidered fabrics used as wall hangings, purses and shawls. Their good humour serves them well, and they employ sign language and a smattering of broken English in their laughter-filled transactions.

I continued travelling south. Between Dali and Xishuangbanna prefecture, the Mekong becomes more accessible. By the time it reaches Jinghong, the Xishuangbanna capital, its evolution renders it ready for commercial traffic. The city is the most influential point on the Mekong in China. It is not only an administrative centre but also a river boarding point for passengers and goods bound for Myanmar and Laos. And, of course, trade and travel flow upriver too. Industrialization has produced

a booming economy and a great influx of visitors, the great majority of whom are Chinese from other provinces.

The architecture here is bland and, despite streets being manicured, Jinghong lacks the timeless charm of Dali. Roads in Jinghong are exceptionally busy, so much so that two-wheeled vehicles now travel in their own designated lanes. However, you leave most of the traffic behind when you cross the new bridge over the Mekong River, now a vital link to an excellent stretch of road, which travels south through the hills. Sadly, though, city factories have caused so much smoke buildup that on some days visibility from Jinghong is too poor for the hills to be seen at all.

Over the bridge, the road to the hills soon leaves the pollution well behind, and there are excellent views of the Mekong River meandering between those hills. On the hillsides and in the valleys, ethnic minorities, such as the Dai, Hani, Jinuo, Lahu and Wa, have made this area their home. Along the hills, as far as the eye can see, are coffee and rubber plantations, banana, orange and pineapple farms, and on the plains below are paddy fields. The Mekong and its waters bring life; these fields very often produce three crops a year; and Xishuangbanna is home to a large proportion of all animal and plant species found in China.

My next stop was on the Mekong River at Ganlanba, a beautiful Dai village. The houses are quite large, open at ground level, timber-built on the upper floor, with gently sloping tiled roofs to ward off the sun, all supported by solid wooden pillars. Spending time in this Dai village, I was drawn to the tranquil 'feel' it possessed. The Dai belong to the T'ai

Above: *Cargo boats on the river at Jinghong.*
Above left: *At sea, most sailors keep a lookout on the water, but this young would-be mariner in Jinghong is trying a dry run on his father's bicycle.*
Opposite: *Watermelon farm, facing Jinghong, the first real town on the Mekong.*

Above: Dai woman going home after work.
Above right: Jinuo woman in traditional costume, in her garden.
Opposite: Menghan Chunman Temple in Ganlanba, a Cultural Revolution casualty but recently restored.

language group and were once part of the Nanzhao and Dali kingdoms. Many of their descendants now live in Thailand, Myanmar and Laos, where they still share a similar culture and language.

'Bamboo House by the Lancang River', a delightful story by Yu Chieu, gives an insight into what life was like for the Dai before the 'integration' of the Cultural Revolution. It is a charming read and briefly recounts some of the changes taking place in the life of Chiang Lan, a young Dai girl narrating her observations. What is clear is that her family started off as very poor, living in a basic bamboo home with hay roofing. Although they all worked very hard to eke out a living, they were very happy and content in their beautiful natural environment. Then came the change, and with it came tiled roofing and, later, timber housing. But Chiang Lan's education was curtailed abruptly to be replaced by working on a production line at the local factory. Ironically though, her failure to complete her studies had no negative impact upon her being able to earn a good living and thus she was able to acquire material comforts in the new society.

Not far from these surroundings the Mekong reaches the border between China and Myanmar. The meeting is brief. Soon, the Mekong River begins to flow between Myanmar and Laos, exchanging its Chinese name for two new ones. To the Lao, the Mekong River is known as the Mae Nam Khong, whilst in Myanmar it is known as the Me Khaun.

Rice drying by the Mekong at Ganlanba. The sandbank, under water during the monsoon season, shows clearly the effect seasonal differences have upon the river.

Myanmar

The Mekong scenery along the border of Myanmar, formerly known as Burma, is absolutely stunning. Along both sides of the river, giant rock formations tower, behind them lush green hills. This is the Mekong at its idyllic best, with almost nothing to impair the view. But although the river is accessible by boat, it continues largely to be shunned by humanity. Here, on the edge of Myanmar's Shan State, all is peaceful. Only a few hilltribe villages appear in the Mekong's landscape and there is little sign of the people who inhabit them, while on the river itself only a few Chinese cargo boats bound for Thailand pass along what in other respects seems like a private waterway.

Kyaingtong, also known as Kengtung, is the nearest Myanmar town or city of any size. Situated regally at very nearly 800 metres above sea level, it lies between the Salween and Mekong rivers, approximately 100 kilometres from each. In Myanmar, the Salween is known as the Thanlwin.

The city of Kyaingtong is built around a natural lake, the Naung Tung, itself a beautiful setting. At almost every turn in the city one sees architectural 'jewels' from various periods, comfortably coexisting. There are Tai–Khün houses perched on slopes and often adjacent to Buddhist temples, there are British colonial buildings, and there are many other architectural treasures from a colourful past, each complementing the other amid the bustle of modern-day living.

As it flows between Myanmar and Laos, the Mekong River passes through wild, rugged, sparsely populated terrain.

In 1993, after several years of self-imposed isolation, Myanmar began to allow foreigners to visit Kyaingtong once more. The opening up of the city has stimulated tourism, encouraging travellers to make the journey, either by road from Mae Sai on the Thai side of the border or by air, and to experience and savour the medley of flavours Kyaingtong holds within. Its relatively slow economic pace and old-fashioned values have contributed to Kyaingtong's success in keeping much of its past intact.

Significantly, Kyaingtong has managed to retain much of the 'Mekong culture' in that it preserves a permeation of the ancient Laotian, Yunnanese and Lanna Thai cultures within its society. Indeed, in many respects, Kyaingtong can be likened to Luang Prabang, the former capital of Laos, for

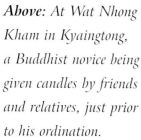

Above: At Wat Nhong Kham in Kyaingtong, a Buddhist novice being given candles by friends and relatives, just prior to his ordination.
Above right: Two young novice nuns on their way to the temple.
Opposite: Local women sell their produce at the market in Kyaingtong.

both places possess a cultured, historical air and grace, and both have largely succeeded in retaining their intrinsic identity.

The Tai–Khün, who make up 80 per cent of the population of Kyaingtong, are believed to be descendants of thirteenth-century migrants from Chiang Mai in Thailand. It is claimed that they are also related to the Shan and Tai–Lue people, with whom they share common beliefs and practise similar traditions.

Shan State is renowned for its diversity of hilltribes. And here in this eastern corner of Shan, particularly in the hills surrounding Kyaingtong, one finds Wa, Shan, Palaung, Akha and Lahu minority groups living in their villages. Every day they travel into Kyaingtong, where they converge upon the marketplace, as much to buy from the locals as to sell their bits and pieces.

*Wat Jong Kham,
with its golden chedi
and htee, overlooking
Naung Tung, the
lake in Kyaingtong.
The htee, an
umbrella-shaped
decoration atop
the chedi, is inlaid
with silver, rubies,
sapphires, diamonds
and jade, and finished
with small gold bells.*

I visited several temples in Kyaingtong and then travelled to Phra That Zom Doi, a hilltop temple about seven kilometres from the city. Traditionally, women are forbidden to enter this sacred sanctuary and, as if to reinforce this, I was treated to a local tale that 'happened not too long ago'. Evidently, one particular woman insisted on setting foot inside the temple and eventually the templekeepers succumbed to her persistent pleas. And then, that very evening, lightning struck and damaged the stupa. Needless to say, I did not venture in but admired instead the wonderful panoramic view of lush green valleys with paddy fields dotting the landscape as far as the eye could see, and clusters of villages surrounded by swaying palms.

At Yang Kong, a village just a few kilometres north of Kyaingtong, I met with some folk who have lived in the village for their entire lives. The village itself was neatly laid out and some of the houses had thatched roofing. Behind one house I observed workmen digging a well in the back garden; many gardens now have wells. Potters displayed their ceramics directly in front of their homes and I was privileged to watch them hard at work, baking the clay.

Above: *Novices walking in file down the street in Kyaingtong. This procession takes place annually in April, during the Myanmar New Year. Some young boys become novice monks for just one or two weeks.*

Opposite: *The stunning nineteenth-century Wat Phra Jao Luang, known also as Maha Myat Muni temple, located in the centre of Kyaingtong.*

On Naung Tung, three locals fish. Each plays his part: one man poles the raft, another draws the net, and the boy is ready with the bucket.

The following day, I visited St. Mary's Convent and Orphanages in Kyaingtong. Run by the Sisters of Charity, St. Mary's also built a school, in 1916, managed at that time by five Italian nuns. The aim of St. Mary's in those days was to educate and care for the orphans, the homeless and the disabled in their charge. Their modern counterparts still operate as the Sisters of Charity, and nowadays also run a small dispensary.

The school, located today at a different site to the original building, which no longer exists, has earned an excellent reputation within the local community, with the result that children from several neighbouring villages travel into Kyaingtong to attend classes here. In addition to normal academic lessons, every one of the 200 children based here is given the added communal responsibilities of gardening, cooking and cleaning.

The achievements from the sisters' collective labour of love are truly impressive. Many hundreds of graduates, several professors, doctors and engineers were first educated here. The school was nationalized in 1965 and, ironically, the sisters have now to raise funds to pay for their orphans to attend!

From Kyaingtong, the border town of Tachilek is 163 kilometres away. There, a bridge over the tiny Sai River links Myanmar to Thailand at Mae Sai. Tachilek derives its importance not only from being a Golden Triangle town but also from serving as an entry point to Myanmar for visitors from Thailand. Plenty of day-trippers seize the opportunity to sightsee and acquire Burmese artifacts from the sprawling market areas.

Above: A Sister of Charity who helps care for orphans at St. Mary's Convent, herself raised there.
Above left: Orphan at St. Mary's Convent.
Opposite: Palaung girls are expected to work in the fields from a young age. When asked her age, the young girl here had no idea.

An extensive selection of just about anything is available, though the goods on sale are mostly of poor quality, many just cheap replicas of the real thing. Incidentally, a replica of the world-famous Shwedagon Pagoda of Yangon has been set atop a knoll in Tachilek and attracts droves of worshippers from Thailand. What Tachilek lacks in originality, it makes up for in the sheer magnitude of its never-ending replicas.

It was interesting to see circular white patches of what looked to be clay on the faces of many local people in the streets of Tachilek. Was this the absolute height of modern border fashion? Not at all — simply a most effective local sunscreen!

The Sai River, separating Tachilek and Mae Sai, flows into the Ruak River which, in turn, flows into the Mekong at the confluence which forms the heart of the Golden Triangle. And it is at this spot that the mighty Mekong River brings three similar cultures from three distinctly different countries together momentarily before leaving Myanmar behind as it gently moves on between the Thai and Lao borders.

Above: In Tachilek, a replica of the Shwedagon Pagoda in Yangon. Many Thais cross the border at Mae Sai to pay respect at this temple.
Opposite: *This hilltribe woman, who lives at St. Mary's Convent, is seen here weaving a basket.*

Laos

I entered Laos at Xieng Kok, a convenient stopover on the border with Myanmar for travellers wanting to catch fast boats down to Houei Xai, from where they may carry on to Thailand or travel to Luang Prabang.

At Xieng Kok I was bowled over by the unsurpassed beauty of the Mekong River, enchanted by the view of it from high above. With no electricity, and having to fetch fresh water from a nearby well at low tide, the enticement of the clear, pure waters proved too strong and I succumbed to the simple pleasure of bathing in its inviting coolness, banishing the oppressive humidity for a while before basking nearby on a fine sandy beach in a small deserted cove. Later, as the sun was setting over the Myanmar hills ahead of me, I sat on some rocks, gazing at the shimmering water until the golden light faded away.

Early next day, local and hilltribe people made their way to the marketplace, where the growing throng soon filled the whole area. There were many products from China, including torches, batteries, hats, shoes, plastic bags, toiletries, biscuits and fruit, including large apples. All were very cheap to buy. Also for sale were old foreign coins, mostly French, many dating back to the early 1900s.

All-encompassing, multi-purpose Lao ferryboat. Earthenware, livestock, engines, food, cement, passengers. You name it, they ferry it!

I decided to venture into hilltribe territory and set off towards Muang Sing in a hired pick-up truck. Sometimes, along the road running parallel to the Ma River, I came across streams that I had to traverse. Other than that, the rest of my journey was less eventful, apart from the

potholes and swirls of dust that enveloped me with each passing vehicle, obscuring what for the rest of the time were spectacular views.

The morning after I arrived in Muang Sing, I discovered a market frequented by minority groups from the surrounding area. Every Saturday, they gather there to sell their wares and to acquire those necessities they cannot produce themselves. It was indeed a colourful jamboree. Bamboo shoots, garlic, corn, rice, meat, and even heads of buffalo were being carted to and from the market. Within a covered section, goods from China were being offered, most of which were the same as those on offer at Xieng Kok, though in Muang Sing the market was bigger, with a wider range of fresh produce. Muang Sing's location close to China makes it ideal for passing trade.

Above: *This Akha girl leads her pony to market, to load it up for the journey home.*
Above right: *Chicken whistle seller at Xieng Kok market.*
Opposite: *Fruits of the Mekong, just landed by Lao fishermen.*

The next morning, I set off on a side trip to Ban Say, 80 kilometres away on the Myanmar border. When I arrived, what I did not expect was the worrying welcome of the headman, peering suspiciously at me — gun in hand! Fortunately, he put it away when my guide assured him that I was a just a harmless visitor. After that he was most helpful in showing us around the village. Late that afternoon, we bade goodbye and returned to Muang Sing.

Walking into Nam Dad Mai village next day, I was fortunate to meet up with Akha villagers working hard to complete the construction of a house for their previous headman. He was considerably wealthy and, befittingly, was building a large Tai–Lue style house on stilts. It took just five days to complete and, when finished, to celebrate its completion,

Hilltribe children at Nam Dad Mai village school, in the hills near Muang Sing town. Wearing a school uniform isn't relevant here. What really counts is having an education.

Above: Akha houses in Nam Dad Mai village.
Opposite: Hilltribe people meet up every Saturday at Muang Sing market, where they buy and sell produce and products. Here, some Akha women consider the benefits of a new acquisition.

three pigs were slaughtered. Ordinarily, one would have sufficed, but as they were two days late in finishing the house, an extra pig had to be sacrificed for each subsequent day's delay. As is customary, the slaughters took place inside the house to ward off evil.

Soon, it was party time and I joined in the revelry. A potent concoction of rice wine was served to the guests, all of whom, whether they liked it or not, were obliged to accept and imbibe at least one measure. Shortly afterwards, an abundance of food was served on banana leaves laid out beautifully on the floor. Towards the end of the evening, a beautiful young girl walked amongst the revellers, soliciting contributions to help defray the cost of the party. When, eventually, I arrived back at my guesthouse and staggered in, it was midnight.

In order to travel on to Houei Xai, it was necessary for me first to go back to Xieng Kok. Once there, I boarded a boat and began to witness the goings-on along the Mekong, which was quite busy with river traffic. Livestock was being transported upstream and down — cows to China, and buffalo to Thailand. Near foaming rapids, strong currents made the boat lurch back and forth but the scenery was so amazing it served to

distract me from impending danger. Magnificent structures of carved stone came into sight with each change of course. Gorges became narrow in parts, and an expert hand was needed to steer clear of rocks that seemed to sprout from nowhere. I had been told about the rapids, but nobody had told me until now that the boat had a new captain! Now I understood why the locals rent speedboats to partake in a pastime of watching boats negotiate the rapids — a source of great amusement for some, though not for our skipper and not for a terrified me!

Houei Xai was known centuries ago as an embarkation point where Yunnanese caravans from China could cross over into Thailand. Today, it seems as busy as ever it must have been, with traders off-loading their wares in makeshift boxes and wicker baskets, cramming them onto small boats by the water's edge. At Houei Xai, those who cross into Laos from Chiang Khong in northwestern Thailand are passing through what is known as the 'Gateway to Indochina'.

At sunrise the next day, I witnessed local people giving alms to Buddhist monks filing down the street. Each monk carried with him a dark wooden bowl — plain, except for a thin gold rim that shimmered when caught by the rays of the sun. The womenfolk and schoolchildren bowed their heads and knelt in humility while making their offerings. Buddhists believe that making merit by such acts in the present life assures a better quality of life in their next incarnation. Theravada Buddhism is the main religion in Laos, just as it is in Thailand, Cambodia and Myanmar.

Above: Wandee, on a ferry at Houei Xai. If ever you travel from here, and a charming Lao woman shares her sticky rice, helps put up your mosquito net, and massages away your boat-induced aches and pains, it's Wandee.
Opposite: Passenger ferry, complete with stowaway.

Rural landscape,
on the way to a
Lao Soung village
between Houei Xai
and Luang Namtha.

My next destination was a village some 70 kilometres away, at an altitude of over 1,000 metres, inhabited by a hilltribe of Lao Soung, or High Lao. Their main cash crop is opium though progressively they are changing to rice and corn farming through the efforts of the Lao–German Development Programme, which also facilitates hilltribe education. From what one could see of the cultivated land below, the programme seems to be working.

Above: Lao Soung love hut for courting couples.
Above right: A young Lao Soung girl on her way to work in the fields.
Opposite: At day's end, the sun's dying rays dance alluringly on the Mekong River.

Arriving at my destination, I came across small bamboo shacks, built on stilts, each dwelling covered by a delightful thatched roof, and each balanced precariously on a slope. These love huts are built specifically for the maidens of the village to entertain their beaus before marriage.

I returned to Houei Xai on the same road whence I had come. Next morning came the much awaited slow boat ride to Luang Prabang, the former royal capital of Laos and one of the most beautifully preserved cities in Southeast Asia. The journey began only when the boat brimmed with cargo of every description and with enough passengers.

The scenery along this stretch of the Mekong is glorious. Lush vegetation prevails on both sides of the river, merging with enormous rocks, and coves and dunes of pure white sand abound. The cool breeze helped the boat along as it followed the natural curves of the river. This was the perfect lazy day. Contentedly, I observed the many aspects of Mekong life, enjoying the scenes of nature and the riverside villages as the

Above: *Here, at Luang Prabang, there are plenty of empty boats around but this woman prefers just to stroll along the riverbank.*

Opposite: *One of the best times to fish is just after daybreak, when the early morning mist shields fishermen from the sun.*

boat passed by. When, finally, the day was drawing to a close, and the sun was just setting, the river turned a dark shade of grey, parted by a rich streak of red where the sun was reflected. The sight was truly glorious!

At the small riverine market town of Pakbeng, we moored. Then, 'stop sleep' was the announcement made. Unprepared for the discomfort of hard, uneven floorboards in the hull, no blanket, no sleeping bag, no pillow, no light, and the weather freezing, by morning I felt as if I had spent the night on an Outward Bound survival test that I had threatened to fail. In fact, I had managed to get a little sleep, only to be woken by the commotion of local people dragging their pigs onto the boats, and transporting their poultry and local produce in bamboo baskets onto the neighbouring boat en route for Luang Prabang market. We set off again shortly afterwards.

There was much to see along the way — elephants roaming along the riverbanks; fishermen in their fragile boats; builders with cement bags, vendors with their produce, and other passengers coming on board where we stopped; and social gatherings on the riverbanks at the end of the day, with whole families of neighbours and friends chatting together, some washing themselves or their clothes in the water while their smiling, waving children frolicked in the river.

The next day, after another uncomfortable night on board, the early morning haze made the landscape appear surreal. In the far distance the mountains stood eerily while the pirogues sat motionless, just as if they were paintings.

Soon the hills were engulfed in mist and I began to recall the words of Louis de Carne:

> *The landscape was at once solemn and imposing. Vapours of milky whiteness stretched over the sky and waters. Nature seemed sleeping, and as if wrapped in a light veil. It attracts one, and absorbs him, dreamily, in spite of himself; ennui invades you at first, then follows an utter indifference. Under the all-powerful constraint of influences so fatal to human personality, thought dies away by degrees like a flame in a vacuum. The East is the true land of Pantheism, and one must have been there to realize the indefinable sensations which almost make Nirvana of the Buddhists comprehensible.* (Louis de Carne, *Travels on the Mekong: Cambodia, Laos and Yunnan.*)

Finally, we arrived in Luang Prabang. This royal city, tucked away in the mountains of northern Laos, at the confluence of the Mekong and the Nam Khan, was unknown to the outside world until the diary of Henri Mouhot, the French explorer, recording his travels in Southeast Asia between 1858–61, was published in London by John Murray in 1864. Luang Prabang was the capital of Lane Xang, meaning million elephants, once one of the largest kingdoms in mainland Southeast Asia. It was established as a royal capital by Fa Ngoum, Lane Xang's first monarch, in 1353, and remained the capital until, in 1563, King Setthathirat moved his capital from Luang Prabang to Vientiane.

Immersed in the placid tranquillity of Luang Prabang, a charming city dominated by the hill known as Phu Si and flanked in part by the majestic Mekong River, it is difficult to visualize what life must have been

Above: Pilgrims on the Mekong approach the sacred caves of Pak Ou.

Opposite: From the mouth of one of the Pak Ou caves, this is the view of the Nam Ou tributary, where it flows into the Mekong, 25 kilometres south of Luang Prabang.

At the conclusion of the
Pimai Lao celebrations
in Luang Prabang,
local dignitaries precede
the replica of the Pra
Bang as it is carried to
its home in the Royal
Palace. Upon arrival,
they will offer their
floral gifts to the
sacred image.

like during its turbulent past. With 32 temples, each of which is at least 200 years old, monks are very much in evidence today, everywhere you go. Fa Ngoum made the golden Buddha image known as the 'Pra Bang' a symbol for the sovereignty of the Lao kingdom of Lane Xang. During the centuries since then, Luang Prabang has remained a religious centre where Laotians from far and wide converge at New Year to pay homage to the Pra Bang from which the city takes its name.

Blessed with good timing, over the next few days I was to witness the celebration of a time-honoured festival. Everyone around me seemed to be buzzing with channelled energy, for this was Pimai Lao, the Lao New Year, and a chance for me to join in the carnival fun and to observe many traditional rituals.

The Mekong River features prominently in the celebrations, the first being the talaat sao, or morning market, held at dawn in the centre of the city, and at one time the largest market in the region, where traders from China, Burma, Siam and Vietnam bartered their wares. Today, traders and other visitors from all over Laos and even further afield flock to trade along a two-kilometre stretch of road. Locally crafted earthenware, baskets, brooms, and food could be found, as could birds in little wooden cages, waiting to be bought and set free, thus making merit for their buyers.

That afternoon, the riverbank was lined with lots of sand-carved stupas decorated with banners on which religious symbols had been

__Above:__ Crowds gather at the Mekong River to celebrate Pimai Lao.
__Above left:__ Baguettes are a daily reminder of the French influence.
__Opposite:__ Sand-carved stupas, bedecked with banners, are a Mekong tradition at Pimai Lao.

Above: Pimai Lao is a great occasion to dress the very smallest in national costume.

Above right: Hmong spectators viewing the Pimai Lao procession from their vantagepoint.

Opposite: In the 'Land of a Million Elephants' these pachyderms are an intrinsic part of Pimai Lao processions.

painted carefully, beckoning the New Year. People, young and old, released fish and tortoises into the river, again to make merit, and splashed joyously in the waters of the great Mekong, a happy ritual symbolizing cleansing and renewal.

Another source of great merriment during Pimai Lao is the bun bang fai, or skyrocket festival. The celebrations begin with the boom of bang fai, or ceremonial rockets, as they are fired high into the sky. Made of wood, bamboo and paper, they are ornamented with the heads of a naga, a mythical water serpent. In Luang Prabang, loud cheers ring out from the launching pad sited at one end of the bank, where people converge in droves to pay homage to the naga, the symbol of their city's guardian spirit, and to partake in the traditional ceremony of welcoming the rainy season. And, having witnessed this event during my visit, that very same night there was rain.

The next day, colourful streams of people started to gather at the roadsides in the city centre. Hours had passed since they set off from their homes, adorned in their traditional finery, the tribal women with children in tow, their men striding forth. Smartly attired city folk were there too. All had one wish in common — to see the parade as it passed by. They were not to be disappointed. It was magical!

The focal point of the parade was the Pra Bang. This image portrays Buddha standing with arms raised forward at the elbows, fingers pointing to the sky to signify supernatural forces that protect those who pay homage. Flanked on either side of the Pra Bang were Luang Prabang's devata luang, or royal tutelary gods, Pou Nheu and Ya Nheu, in large

startlingly red sacred masks with a profusion of coarse mane streaming along their bodies. It is said that these two gods created the earth and planted the gourds that gave life to mankind. This dramatic and divine entourage provided the focal point of the procession, which included local dignitaries and many groups of local people in colourful costumes.

The spectators lining the route looked on with a mixture of emotions and reactions that verged from silent awe to screams of excitement. As soon as the parade had passed, the crowd followed immediately. The farther along the route the parade progressed, the more crowded the throng following the procession became.

My final destination in Luang Prabang was a mound overgrown with vegetation. By the banks of the Nam Khan, with a view across the crystal clear water to the hill beyond, lay the tomb of Henri Mouhot. Standing there, and remembering the dedication to his task which cost him his life, I felt very sad as I thought about the lonely manner of his passing.

Leaving Luang Prabang for Vientiane, the capital of Laos, the Mekong River flows placidly towards Chiang Khan on the border between Laos and Thailand, passing between beautiful scenery along its banks, but the river also has a darker side. In some parts during the dry season, when the water is at its lowest, exposed or shallow rocks can make navigation extremely perilous for all river traffic. After the small town of

Above: Wat Xieng Thong, built in 1560, one of Luang Prabang's most beautiful temples.
Above left: Buddha image in Wat Saen Soukharam.
Opposite: Giving rice to monks making their morning alms rounds.

Fishing boats at
Luang Prabang.
The impression is
of a misty morning.
But, in fact, the boats
are set against a haze
of smoke caused by local
farmers practising their
slash-and-burn method
of agriculture.

Above: *That Luang is Vientiane's most important monument and is the holiest Buddhist site in Laos. Situated on a hill on the edge of the city, its golden spire dominates the surrounding area.*
Opposite: *The ornate entrance doors of That Luang.*

Muang Tha Deua is passed, there is little to stop for until Pak Lai is reached. Pak Lai itself has little of interest in its own right but it offers a break from the long river journey from Luang Prabang to Vientiane, conveniently placed as it is halfway between the two cities. From Pak Lai, the Mekong moves towards the Thai border, which it reaches at Chiang Khan. Then, once more marking the border between Laos and Thailand, the river travels northeastwards until it swings to the southeast and flows on down to Vientiane.

On first impression, Vientiane reminded me of the Bangkok I had known from my childhood in the '50s. With its pretty setting alongside the Mekong River, it has an unmistakable 'cowboy town' feel about it, and a lovely unhurried pace. There were no neon signs to blot the view of charming old shophouses selling everything from cakes to stupas, nor spoil the atmosphere of numerous 'coffee shops' where the locals get together for quick noodle or rice dishes, as have generations before them. During the evening, there is not much traffic on the roads. Those who do travel seem to prefer various forms of two- or three-wheelers, some motorized, some manual.

The gate by That Luang, just before sunset.

Vientiane today is clearly in a state of flux, yet the inhabitants, gentle, soft-spoken and traditional, still manage to appear unfazed by it all. A French restaurateur I chatted to, who had been based there for 15 years, declared that the essence of Laos was not reflected in her capital. Nodding in agreement, having travelled to Muang Sing and through Luang Prabang, I understood exactly what he meant.

Two places of real significance in Vientiane, probably reflecting the Laos of a more grand era are That Luang and Wat Sisaket. That Luang, an impressive temple possessing a splendid golden spire, looks especially magnificent at dusk when it reflects the diffused light of the setting sun. It is the most holy of all Buddhist monuments in Laos. Wat Sisaket, the oldest temple in Vientiane, is very attractive though badly in need of restoration. Built in 1818, it is an architectural jewel, with an exquisitely detailed ceiling.

From Vientiane, the Mekong flows beneath the Thai–Lao Friendship Bridge, which links both countries by road. Downriver the Mekong is joined by its Lao tributary, the Nam Ngum, and the extra volume of water causes the Mekong to widen here. Continuing to define the border between Laos and Thailand, the Mekong passes through some marvellous hill landscapes, especially between Tha Khaek and Nakhon Phanom, on the Lao and Thai sides of the border respectively.

Tha Khaek, with its small river port, is a quiet trading town waiting for the building of a bridge across the Mekong. The bridge is in the National Plan for Laos but no one seems in a hurry to implement it. When they do, this benign town will spring to life.

Above: *Monks, in the compound of Wat Sisaket in Vientiane.*
Opposite: *One of many Buddha images in the cloisters of Wat Sisaket.*

One hundred kilometres downriver from Tha Khaek is Savannakhet, an important river port, known in Laos as the gateway to the south. Despite its importance as a trading centre with Thailand, it retains a rural charm that has long since disappeared from most other towns and cities in the region. In its streets, cattle, goats and chickens roam freely. Just as at Tha Khaek, Savannakhet awaits its bridge across the Mekong.

Just south of the small Thai town of Khong Chiam, the Mun River, a major Thai tributary, flows into the Mekong. Soon the Mekong travels solely in Lao territory, forging its course through dense forests in the province of Champasak and meandering for 30 kilometres until it reaches Pakse, where the Mekong is met by the Se Don River. This bustling, noteworthy Mekong town was where I began to trace the last leg of the river's journey through Laos.

Pakse, capital of Champasak province, can best be described as a haphazard blend of old and new. A bridge across the Mekong was under construction at the time of my visit and eventually will provide a link between Pakse and Thailand.

The province of Champasak was part of the Cambodian Angkor Empire between the tenth and thirteenth centuries. Today very little remains to remind of this forgotten age, except for the impressive and important archaeological ruins of Wat Phu, which is believed to have been built around 800 years ago.

Above: *The crumbling ruins of Wat Phu Champasak in southern Laos.*
Above left: *An entrance to the sanctuary at Wat Phu Champasak.*
Opposite: *From Pha Taem cliff, the Mekong with Laos beyond.*

Above: Despite the obvious dangers of the waters at the Phapheng Falls in southern Laos, local people fish from rocks in the river and then carry their catch back across apparently makeshift bridges, such as the rickety contraption these boys are negotiating.
Opposite: Casting the net into the foaming, seething waters at Phapheng Falls.

In the extreme south of Laos, the Mekong has many islands, the largest of which is Don Khong, approximately eight kilometres wide and sixteen kilometres long. The river in this area attains a gulf-like girth of fourteen kilometres and is full of islands. During the dry season the area becomes know as Si Phan Don, or 'the 4,000 islands'.

But not to be surpassed, close to the border with Cambodia, are the Khone Falls. Split into two spectacular cascades, the Phapheng Falls and the Somphamit Falls, together they constitute the Mekong River's largest waterfalls and most breathtaking spectacle. Stupendous in every respect, every sensation at the Khone Falls is heightened by the presence of their immensely powerful cascades of swirling, frothing, gushing jade and emerald green jets of water.

The Khone Falls make a fantastic grand finale to the river's journey through Laos. Soon, the majestic Mekong regains its composure and settles down again, flowing swiftly yet quietly through the small town of Veun Khan, before moving into Cambodia.

106

Thailand

And so it was that I began the journey in my motherland, in the infamous Golden Triangle, whose very name is synonymous with the world's most productive opium-growing region. However, less widely publicized is that it is here, at the confluence of the Mekong and Ruak rivers, that the borders of Thailand, Laos and Myanmar come together and form a triangular junction from which the name of the area is derived.

In Chiang Rai province, Sop Ruak, little more than a village but very, very busy, is officially the centre of the Golden Triangle, which defines an area incorporating surrounding towns within the three countries. From a designated site, high on a hill, I was able to appreciate the view of the point where the three countries meet. This view I shared with numerous other visitors, who stood in line to be photographed under a sign reading 'Welcome to the Golden Triangle'. Here also, one had to contend with the bustle of stall vendors trying to tout their souvenirs. A shrine, perched on a higher site, in close proximity to the viewing spot, houses the deities who are ever watchful of the river. Offerings of flower garlands are made by the local people in gratitude for guidance and protection received.

Further away, atop an even higher hill, stands a magnificent golden Buddha, towering over the Golden Triangle and serving as the principal guardian of this stretch of river. The local people believe also that it ensures friendship between the three nations below. The view from here

At Sop Ruak on the Mekong River, a Thai man preparing his boat before ferrying the day's first passengers across to Laos.

Above: *The Phra Buddha Palanuphap Lakmahaan statue, overlooking the Mekong River at Sop Ruak, signifies the friendship between Thailand, Laos and Myanmar, and shared Buddhist beliefs.*
Opposite: *The Ruak River joining the Mekong at the heart of the Golden Triangle.*

is splendid and, away from all the crowds, one truly can appreciate the stillness and experience the sheer magnetism of the place.

There was very little river activity that day and, when I inquired as to why, I was told that the 'Myanmar side' had closed the border to all traffic — except that which was bound for their disproportionately large casino complex that to me seemed the only thing marring an otherwise picture-perfect view.

In an effort to educate the local populace and visitors to this region about the history of the opium trade, and to dispel any misconceptions about Thailand's stand against associated illegal activities, 'The House of Opium' is well worth a visit. There is so much to see and learn at this quaint little museum, which displays an amazing trove of opium-related 'treasures', ranging from elaborate and beautiful illustrations showing the cultivation of the poppy plant to the various processes involved in the production of the hallucinatory substance. There are pipes of every description, graduated animal-shaped weights, various brass and wooden containers, and a multitude of tools and utensils on display, complete with comprehensive explanations of their purpose. Admittedly, similar items have found their way into my home somehow, as decorative pieces, but prior to visiting this museum I had not realized for what purpose they had been used originally.

From Sop Ruak I made my way to Mae Sai, the northernmost town in Thailand. This busy trading centre is right on the border with Myanmar, and the bridge across the Sai River serves as a crossing point

between the two countries. In contrast to the bustling activity of Mae Sai, the town of Tachilek, on the Myanmar side of the river, is relatively quiet.

As the Sai River flows towards the Mekong, it marks the border until it flows into the Ruak River which, in turn, joins the Mekong, close to Sop Ruak, the point of the Golden Triangle where Thailand, Myanmar and Laos all meet. Mae Sai is a good centre from which to visit the Golden Triangle villages of Doi Tung and Doi Mae Salong.

Away from the towns, many areas of the Golden Triangle that are used for poppy cultivation are so remote and inaccessible that in the past they have proved to be virtually ungovernable. For several generations, hilltribe farmers have lived on these forested mountain slopes, growing poppies. Originally, very many of these farmers practised slash-and-burn agriculture, eking out a meagre existence. However, growing poppies for the opium trade has proved more lucrative. So it is unsurprising that efforts to combat the opium trade have often met with resistance. Nevertheless, the government of Thailand has continued to conduct an arduous and dedicated offensive against the unacceptable aspects of opium-connected activity.

Above: The beautiful landscaped garden of Her Royal Highness Somdej Phra Srinakharinthara Baromrachachonnani, the late Princess Mother, within the grounds of her royal residence at Doi Tung.
Opposite: Doi Chang Moob, near Doi Tung, especially beautiful at sunset. On a clear day, both Myanmar and Laos can be seen from here.

Above: An Akha beadseller at Chiang Rai's night bazaar.
Above right: Akhara, a young Akha girl from Doi Mae Salong.
Opposite: Near Doi Mae Salong, a young teaworker fashioning the handle of a tea-harvesting implement, behind him a tea plantation.

In the past ten years, Thailand's continued efforts have begun to reap good results, credited not least to numerous development programmes that in general have been well-received by the hillpeople and to royal patronage of many projects. One particularly special project, initiated by Her Royal Highness Somdej Phra Srinakharinthara Baromrachachonnani, the late Princess Mother, is at Doi Tung. It was the exemplary vision of Her Royal Highness to 'cultivate the people' and her conviction of spirit gently to coax them away from activities of an illegal nature. Through her genuine love, nurturing and enormous commitment, many of the hilltribes were convinced to embark instead on cash crop cultivation and the utilization of modern methods of farming. Alongside the creation of an impressive garden, which the royal residence overlooks in Doi Tung, a separate project to promote and market hilltribe crafts — embroidery, woven products, silverware and ornaments — has been launched successfully throughout the country. The proceeds from sales go directly to bettering the lives of the hillpeople and ensuring a brighter future for their young.

These programmes have helped also to establish healthy integration through commerce and sometimes intermarriage with the mainstream population as is the case at Doi Mae Salong. This thriving village, perched high on the hills of Chiang Rai province, owes its existence to Yunnanese soldiers who fled there from China after the Communists defeated the Nationalists in 1949. Although at one time they were extremely active in the opium trade, these northern migrants were encouraged by the Thai authorities to begin cultivating other crops and

have succeeded to the point where they are now considered to have created a model environment. Today, acres of coffee, tea, strawberry, lychee and highland crops thrive in neatly terraced plots that dot the landscape beautifully, as far as the eye can see. It was enough of a treat to drive through the narrow, winding lanes into the village just to witness these industrious folk going about their business. Their houses are immaculate and a profusion of colour from flowers catches the eye at every turn. One can see clearly that they have established themselves economically.

A charming woman who runs a teahouse was happy to show me her backyard, where a family of Akha was employed to sort tealeaves. Within the compound there was also a processing plant, equipped with heavy machinery, and she invited me to enjoy the view from her balcony, which overlooks her plantation. The quality of the tea produced in Mae Salong is quite superb and certainly deserves sampling.

In Chiang Rai city, signs of recent development flashed with every neon light, hotel, restaurant and travel agent lining the busy roads. These same roads or, rather, pavements become littered with vegetables and fruit every afternoon when hillpeople sell the produce from their farms at the street market. The night bazaar is a colourful jamboree of locals, hillpeople and western tourists engaged in playful banter and barter. I saw goods of every description from all over Southeast Asia being displayed for sale at the 'best price'. Hillpeople really have caught on that a price game should precede every sale, and as soon as the exchange starts they are quick to smile, revealing their teeth, blackened from betel nut stains.

Above: The 70-metre-high Khun Korn Falls, Chiang Rai.
Above left and opposite: *A group of boy scouts and girl guides at the Khun Korn Falls. Within a few minutes, all were splashing about in the water.*

Many visitors use Chiang Rai as a starting point from which to explore nearby hilltribe villages or beauty spots, either on foot, by bike or in a tour van. I decided to venture to the picturesque Khun Korn Falls, located at 1,250 metres above sea level. These 70-metre-high falls were spectacular, and even more fun when a group of scouts and guides from a nearby school arrived on their excursion and, with little hesitation, jumped straight into the chilling pool at the base of the falls.

The city's finest temple is Wat Phra Kaeo, originally known as Wat Pa-Hi'er. Its name change occurred after its stupa was struck by lightning in 1434. The damage caused revealed that the stupa contained the Emerald Buddha, Thailand's most sacred Buddha image, which now resides at Wat Phra Kaeo in Bangkok. In order to replace the image after many centuries of absence from Chiang Rai and, at the same time, to mark the 90th birthday of Her Royal Highness The Princess Mother, a replica of the Emerald Buddha was made, which Her Royal Highness named 'Phraphuttaratanakorn Nawutiwatsanusornmongkhon', meaning 'The Lord Buddha is the Source of the Three Gems of Buddhism'. And so there is now, once again, an Emerald Buddha image at Wat Phra Kaeo in Chiang Rai.

My next stopover was at Chiang Saen, birthplace of the founder of the Lanna Kingdom, King Mangrai, whose grandson, King Saen Phu, founded the Chiang Saen Kingdom of which Chiang Saen became the capital. It is clear that recently the town has enjoyed an injection of funds for development, with the appearance of newly constructed blocks of

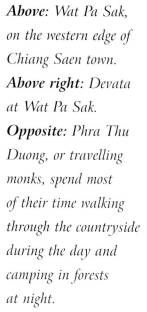

Above: Wat Pa Sak, on the western edge of Chiang Saen town.
Above right: Devata at Wat Pa Sak.
Opposite: Phra Thu Duong, or travelling monks, spend most of their time walking through the countryside during the day and camping in forests at night.

low-rise shophouses along the river's edge, in stark contrast to the town's ancient stupas, chedis, and ruins of its old city walls. Once an important river port of the Mekong, today it appears to have slowed down considerably bar a few cargo boats being loaded with instant noodles bound for Laos.

King Mangrai was born in Chiang Saen in 1239 and established his kingdom after uniting the warring, bickering lords of the north into one region, and one ruler: himself. A small branch of the National Museum, not far from the town centre, reminds of Chiang Saen's grander days and displays an impressive collection of Lanna pottery. It also contains many interesting exhibits relating to the various hilltribes — their modes of dress, patterns of weaving and lifestyles.

Close to the museum, but standing just outside the city ramparts in a marvellous setting of teak forest, is Wat Pa Sak. Much of the original fine stucco work is no longer in evidence, though some naga and garuda fragments still exist. However, the niches around the base of the main chedi contain restored Devatas (female deities) and Buddha images. Fortunately, the Fine Arts Department of Thailand is pursuing restoration work to preserve this ancient monument.

Every April, sleepy Chiang Saen wakes with a jolt as the annual Songkran, or Thai New Year, celebrations take place. At this time, all the local villages participate in the revelry, and villagers from China, Myanmar and Laos come to join in the fun, too. A full programme of events is organized, including individual country traditional dance and beauty contests, and Myanmar and Thai crews race each other in their dragon boats.

Above: A Chiang Saen beauty-contest hopeful, waiting to go on stage.
Above left: Paying respect to Buddha images at Songkran.
Opposite: Men dressed in traditional Lanna style and carrying ceremonial banners in the Songkran Bai Si procession at Chiang Saen.

*Above: Two young
Muay Thai adversaries
battle for honours in
an open-air ring beside
the Mekong River
at Chiang Saen.
In Muay Thai,
or 'Thai boxing',
any part of the
body, except the
head, may be used
to strike an opponent.*
Opposite: *Preparing
to participate in the
Songkran parade in
Chiang Saen.*

A few kilometres away from Chiang Saen lies the Hmong hilltribe village of Kiew Kang. I had been warned that these people were not entirely comfortable with outsiders and valued their privacy enormously. To photograph some of the scenes I was witnessing might encroach upon their lives. I found myself in a quandary as to whether or not to go by instinct and just approach the first friendly face, smile pleadingly and request a photograph. In fact, that is what I did and it felt wonderful to be granted privy to their lives that day. I was even invited to take pictures in their village school which, incidentally, is run by Thai border police personnel who double as teachers. The children were more than amused to see me, not least because, unknown to me, a giant grasshopper had found its way onto my shoulder. They thought this was hilarious, of course. And when, eventually, I saw the object of their noisy amusement, their hilarity became contagious and I laughed heartily too.

My next destination was Chiang Khong, which is just 55 kilometres downriver from Chiang Saen. This small town is faced on the Laos side by the even smaller town of Houei Xai, known familiarly as the 'Gateway to Indochina'. Though small, Chiang Khong is a busy border town, with

Above: Cockerels, a common sight in many of the mountain villages, here seen at Kiew Kang.
Opposite: White Hmongs at Kiew Kang village. Traditionally, the women shave almost all of their head. Here a mother has just finished collecting some fir branches that will be used to make brooms.

boats crossing back and forth across the river, full of goods destined for the country opposite.

Below Chiang Khong, high on a mountain overlooking the Mekong, is the vertical rock face known as Phu Hin Chee Fah. At over 1,600 metres above sea level, this spot is famed for the spectacular views it affords at sunrise. At daybreak, the rolling hills which border Thailand and Laos are at their most impressive as the early morning clouds, known locally as the 'Sea of Clouds', gently but firmly float over the Mekong River below. It is a strange feeling to have one's feet firmly planted on the ground yet be looking down at the clouds instead of up at them.

Soon, downriver from Phu Hin Chee Fah, the Mekong drifts away from the Thai–Lao border until turning sharp east towards Luang Prabang, deep in the heart of Laos. From Luang Prabang, the river travels almost directly south until it reaches Thailand again near the town of Chiang Khan, in Loei province. Travelling northeastwards, it defines the border between Thailand and Laos once more.

Downriver from Chiang Khan lies the sacred temple sanctuary of Wat Hin Maak Peng, situated in an absolutely perfect setting.

Overlooking the Mekong River, its grounds descend onto smooth, giant boulders at the water's edge. The monks here have a paradise on earth in which to meditate.

All was still and quiet as I began to witness a sacred rite. I had been invited to participate in the proceedings to follow but declined, preferring instead to pay my respects in silent prayer. Three monks in saffron robes, three relatives of the deceased and the boatman from whose vessel the ceremony was being conducted made up the seven persons required for the ritual to take place. As I watched, the boat stopped close to a massive riverside rockface, and the ashes were sprinkled slowly and deliberately onto the Mekong River. Soon the ceremony was over and the mourners were back on land. From my vantagepoint I stood transfixed for a while, gazing down as the sprinklings of flower petals and ashes moved slowly away in swirls.

As I travelled on, scenes of tobacco farmers tending their crops, their womenfolk drying the darkened leaves on flat, woven bamboo trays by the roadside or sometimes letting them hang in the ground-floor space beneath their stilted houses, were a common sight. Driving on, as I began

***Above:** Hmong woman on the top of Phu Hin Chee Fah, Chiang Rai province.*
__Opposite:__ Phu Hin Chee Fah. From here, at an altitude of over 1,600 metres, the view of the famous 'Sea of Clouds' at sunrise is spectacular, obscuring completely the Mekong River below.

Below Wat Hin Maak Peng, 64 kilometres northwest of Nong Khai, monks perform an ash-sprinkling ceremony on the Mekong River.

to draw closer to Si Chiang Mai in Nong Khai province, I saw houses with, outside them, bamboo racks full of translucent rice-paper discs basking in the hot midday sun. Later, I was told that a large proportion of Lao and Vietnamese local residents gain their livelihood from the manufacture of these spring roll wrappers. Indeed, Si Chiang Mai is the world's leading exporter of this unique product.

In due course, we arrived in the town of Nong Khai. Since the completion of the Thai–Lao Friendship Bridge in 1994, the town has become a veritable hub of activity, with much construction under way, and border traffic and trade have increased significantly. This is the only completed bridge to span the Mekong River between Thailand and Laos, and for those from Laos it provides excellent communication links to every corner of Thailand. As a result, Nong Khai now attracts many more visitors to the region and more residents too. An increase in tourism is reflected by the numerous quality hotels, bars, restaurants and craft shops sprouting at every turn. Business is thriving in the centre, while along the waterfront the olde worlde Chinese and French colonial-style buildings are fast making way for their modern counterparts, which are almost always less attractive. Fortunately, the embankment has far from lost its charm, with several temples along it remaining permanent fixtures in the changing landscape.

The view of the famous Phra That Nong Khai, or Phra That Klang Nam ('stupa in the middle of the river') as it is locally known, depends

Above: A farm labourer collecting tobacco leaves at Tha Bo, Nong Khai province.
Above right: Buddha image in a field at Tha Bo.
Opposite: Tobacco leaves being transported to the tobacco factory.

very much on the time of year. Close to the centre of the Mekong River, for most of the year it lies submerged. Then, as the water level drops during the dry season, it emerges for all to see and is quickly garlanded with banners and pennants, providing an altogether unexpected and extraordinary sight.

One of the broadest sections of the Mekong valley is located below Nong Khai, where the Nam Ngum tributary joins the river from the Lao side. On the Thai side, growing in abundance along the silt-enriched fertile banks of the river are tomato and tobacco plants, and cultivated plots dot the landscape, creating a tapestry of green and earthy hues.

Archaeological discoveries made during 1966 in the sleepy village of Ban Chiang in Udon Thani province subsequently prompted academics to include the Khorat Plateau, in the Mekong Basin, as one of the world's probable cradles of civilization. An excavated mould in which bronze axes were cast dates back more than five thousand years, indicating that sophisticated bronze artifacts were being made in Southeast Asia as early as, and possibly even earlier than, anywhere else in the world. Other archaeological finds made at Ban Chiang suggest that there was also

Above: Girl at Nong Khai market selling flowers for temple offerings.
Opposite: Monks walking in the grounds of Wat Khaek on the eastern outskirts of Nong Khai town. An unusual Hindu–Buddhist wat, established in the late 1970s, it contains a garden strangely mixing images and statues of the two religions.

Above: During 1972, excavations at Wat Pho Si Nai in Ban Chiang, Udon Thani province, revealed ancient burial pits containing local ceramics. Deliberately broken into mere fragments at the time of burial, they have been dated as made between 3000 BC and AD 200.

Opposite: Songkran. What better fun than a soaking in the sun!

ironworking and considerable pottery-making technology in the same region around three thousand years ago.

One of the best places from which to enjoy a romantic view of the Mekong River, with the mountains of Laos as a backdrop, is Nakhon Phanom, particularly on a slightly misty day. Across the water, the lush green trees and profusion of natural vegetation, as yet untouched by human development, served to remind me of what it must have been like on my side of the bank in times past.

It was towards the end of the cool, dry season and the water level was low. Where sandbanks had eaten into the river, vast stretches of 'beach' had been created, as had islands in the middle of its course. It looked as if I could wade across to the quiet shores of Laos. Locals make the most of this naturally reclaimed land to cultivate peanuts, flowers and vegetables, leasing plots of land from the local authorities, free of charge.

Fishermen who had pitched tent at the far side of a sandbank complained to me of their meagre catch being the norm for this time of year. This April evening was particularly cold and they stood huddled in front of a fire. They would spend the night here and at dawn would search

the shallow river for fish. The setting sun cast its reflection on the water, now just a narrow strip trapped between large expanses of sand.

I travelled south from Nakhon Phanom until I reached the town of That Phanom. Here is found one of the most revered shrines along the Mekong, Wat Phra That Phanom, which is believed to contain a relic of the Buddha. Thais from all over the country make it a point to come to this temple, the most sacred in the Northeast, to make special prayers and to walk around the central Lao-style chedi, 52 metres high, its spire decorated with 110 kilograms of gold. Some archaeologists set its age at about 1,500 years. Strange though it may seem, this temple is second only to That Luang in Vientiane in being revered by the people of Laos, despite the fact that it lies across the Mekong River, in Thailand! Reinforcing the Lao influence here, just upriver from That Phanom, a twice-weekly morning market full of pigs, Lao fabric, herbal medicines and forest plants is run by Lao traders who cross over into Thailand.

On the way down to Mukdahan, there are occasional stretches of rapids, sometimes with rocky outcrops from which to view them. I stopped awhile at the Khaeng Kha Bao rapids, where local people gather in clusters to picnic. The views from above, access to the rippling water's edge, and a friendly atmosphere created by the families who visit seem certain to lure more and more day-trippers to this beauty spot.

Mukdahan is another riverine town, with fine scenic views. The town is a Thai–Lao trading centre known for its Talaat Indochine, or Indochinese Market, where all manner of goods from Thailand and Laos

Above: *A nun at Wat Phra That Phanom, That Phanom, clearing up debris of spent candles left behind by visitors. Pilgrims from all over Thailand and Laos travel to worship at this holy place.*
Opposite: *Wat Phra That Phanom is one of the most revered shrines in northeast Thailand.*

are traded daily near the pier. Unlike many marketplaces I've visited, this one felt very calm despite being busy.

Pha Taem, situated in the Khong Chiam district of Ubon Ratchathani province, is an impressive, high, sheer cliff from the top of which one is able to admire a breathtaking panorama of the Mekong River as it meanders through some of Thailand's lushiest and finest countryside. But topping even that, Pha Taem also features prehistoric colour paintings etched along its face. Following the signs pointing the way to the 'Painting Cliff', I walked along and up a steep and sometimes narrow trail before encountering paintings of elephants, giant Mekong catfish known as pla buk, fish traps, people, designs, and many handprints, most probably of the artists themselves. Pha Taem is a conservation area and has been designated a national park. After viewing these ancient works of art, I travelled just a few kilometres from Pha Taem to an area known as Sao Chaliang, where strange stone clusters, looking remarkably like giant mushrooms, stand tall in the surrounding countryside.

Above: *The giant stone 'mushrooms' of Sao Chaliang.*
Above right: *At Pha Taem, prehistoric cliff paintings.*
Opposite: *Fisherman, precariously perched on his boat, Khong Chiam.*

Khong Chiam itself is situated on a picturesque peninsula formed by the confluence of the Mun and Mekong rivers, fondly referred to as 'The Two-Colour River'. The peninsula has become a popular viewing spot from where to witness the merging of the muddy-coloured Mekong with the clear blue Mun. Just before the Mun reaches the Mekong, it flows close to the beautiful Sirinthon reservoir where fisherman lay their

Above: Khong Chiam. When the schoolbus is full, there's always room for more.

Opposite: At Khong Chiam, old man fixing his boat. Despite pleas from his family for him and his wife to go and live in the city, they are happy here, where they always want to be — by the Mekong River.

traps in tranquil waters, and elsewhere by its shores happy parents and children swim and enjoy their water play.

At Khong Chiam it is possible to hire a boat to travel back upriver to view the spectacular cliff at Pha Taem from a different perspective. Travelling on the Mekong in a narrow boat is idyllic, and little compares to that feeling of being an integral part of the surroundings.

Just upriver from Khong Chiam, the banks were busy with farmers tending their crops, planted right to the river's edge. All along are irrigation pumps and pipelines, making their way to the thirsty crops along the banks. And just as a precaution, the farmers also use watering cans during the dry season for their salad vegetables, coriander and mint.

After disembarking, I engaged in conversation with the wife of a seventy-year-old grandfather fisherman who was hard at work fixing his boat. As I listened to her, she gave me much insight into the local community and their activities. She told me that while her husband was fishing, she played her part in contributing to their combined income by farming vegetables and selling them at the local market. With obvious pride, she told me about her children. All had been to college and then to university. She smiled as she added that each one of them was now successful in business and all, individually, would like her and her husband to go and live with them. But this was her home. Growing and nurturing her vegetables was a way of life. And for her husband, fishing was his way of life, too. But more importantly, their way of life continued to bring them happiness and fulfillment. Why change? For they are content, just as they are — on the banks of the Mekong River.

Cambodia

After the mighty Khone Falls in Laos, the Mekong quietens down and then crosses the border into Cambodia. When it reaches the Sambor Rapids, between Stung Treng and Kratie, its pace quickens substantially. Sambor, an ancient trading post, was visited in the seventeenth century by Gerrit Van Wusthoff, the Dutch merchant venturer. In 1866, the members of the expedition of Ernest Doudart de Lagrée and Francis Garnier, endeavouring to determine how far the Mekong was navigable upriver from the Mekong Delta, stayed at Sambor en route. It is still a matter of debate today as to whether or not the challenge of navigating this stretch of the Mekong River, with its rather unpredictable course of rock-infested waters, is worth the risk. I was not brave enough and took instead to the calmer stretches.

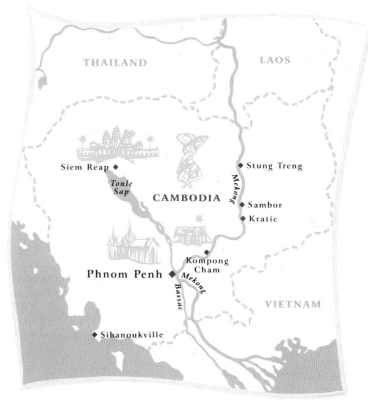

I spent a few hours in Kompong Cham, one of the largest towns in Cambodia, situated on the Mekong River between Kratie and Phnom Penh. A flourishing trading centre during the French colonial era, the legacy of commercial prosperity remains in evidence today. The town retains fragments of its colonial charm through the classic architecture of its buildings.

By interacting with the local residents, you begin to understand their arduous struggle to better their lives. Most things are in short supply. The psah, or market, is a shadow of its former self, the produce available being but a fraction of the display abundantly spread across the market

Ferryboats on the Mekong at Kompong Cham. The one in the foreground carries cargo on the lower deck and passengers above.

Above: Girls, whiling away the time in Kompong Cham.
Above right: A reminder of the architecture of French colonial days.
Opposite: The bridge under construction across the Mekong at Kompong Cham will link traffic to and from Laos and Vietnam, on its eastern side, with traffic to and from Sihanoukville and Thailand, on its western side. At this pivotal point, Cambodia stands to gain all round.

square in times past. And there aren't all that many takers. I purchased some oranges imported from Thailand and offered one to my driver who politely declined, saying 'fruit is luxury — only for rich people'. Little is taken for granted here, the inhabitants dotted along the riverbanks in shanty housing eking out a mere existence. There is so much resting on the opening of a Japanese-financed bridge across the Mekong which will complete the highway route from Bangkok to Ho Chi Minh City, via Kompong Cham, bringing long-awaited trade and increased prosperity to this part of Cambodia. At the time of my visit, the project was well under way and the main hotel of the city brimmed with activity.

Driving out of Kompong Cham, a few kilometres along the road to Phnom Penh I stopped to inspect what looked to be old ruins. Originally a Mahayana-Buddhist temple but reconsecrated for Theravada-Buddhist worship in the fifteenth century, Wat Nokor Bayon is built of sandstone and laterite. Through a loudspeaker, at full blast, the voice of a monk preaching assaulted the ears. Perhaps that was why his congregation seemed so restless. Meanwhile, trying not to disturb their worship, I roamed the small courtyards and alcoves, admiring the statues.

Then I looked again at those gathered. What was lovely to see was that it seemed as if the entire community was there to rally round their spiritual leader, even though it appeared some were only half listening. As I left, I could see nearby the more modern part of the monastery, where the monks lived, their saffron robes hanging outside in rows to dry.

The drive from Kompong Cham to the city of Phnom Penh, the capital of Cambodia, was pleasant and scenic. The roads are in pretty good shape and the views are delightful in all directions. On either side of the road could be seen row upon row of colourful wooden houses perched

on stilts, each with a distinctive three-tier roofing structure. Some of the shutters and blinds are a bright shade of blue and make a striking contrast to the flat, arid plains of the surrounding countryside. Palms dot the landscape as far as the eye can see, interspersed with rubber trees.

I could tell by the transformation in the scenery that I was fast approaching Phnom Penh. Brightly illuminated restaurants now lined the road for a few kilometres, and then I crossed over the Cambodian–Japanese Friendship Bridge, which spans the Tonle Sap River at the edge of Phnom Penh. Originally the ill-fated Chruoy Changvar Bridge, it was destroyed by the Khmer Rouge in 1975, and repaired only in 1993 with Japanese funding. Although dusk made the cultivated farmland along the banks of the Tonle Sap River barely visible, Phnom Penh by night looked almost regal. Partially lit colonial buildings stood majestically on long, wide, tree-lined boulevards. The embankment makes an especially pretty sight and is a hub of activity by nightfall. It seemed as though every design of two- and three-wheeler was out to moonbathe. Moving at snail's pace, each with a full complement of passengers, whole families balanced precariously.

That night I relaxed in the ambient surroundings of the Foreign Correspondents Club of Cambodia from where, in its pleasantly breezy upstairs bar, I looked out across the Mekong River. What must it be like to be here during Bon Om Tuk, the Water and Moon festival, I wondered? The festival marks the end of the rainy season, when the monsoon waters begin to escape from the Great Lake and flow down the Tonle Sap River. The highlight of the festival is the dragon boat racing

Above and opposite: Wat Nokor Bayon, just outside Kompong Cham town, is the most well-known religious monument in the area.
Above left: Pick-up trucks transport all manner of goods. In this instance, one might be forgiven for thinking this is some kind of circus act.

with hundreds of crews competing, some for glory, most just for fun. It was too good a place to leave so I checked in for the night.

The next morning, when I ventured out, everything looked and felt completely different in the light of day. On foot, the pace is slow, and one sees in so much more detail than when being transported at some speed. The same elegant buildings of the night before seemed rather less majestic now, for most of them were in need of more than just a coat of paint. Nevertheless, I could see why Phnom Penh was once acclaimed the most charming city in Indochina. Alas, that reputation was more than thirty years ago. Since then the ravages of war and poverty have taken their toll.

Above: The Mekong, in the background, about to be joined by the Tonle Sap River.
Above right: Monks by the Tonle Sap River.
Opposite: Sisowath Quay, Phnom Penh, quiet on weekdays, busy at night and weekends.

Despite myriad restaurants, hotels and bustling market squares, the deep wound has yet to heal. I confronted it daily in some form or another, whether it was the nun fighting to hold back her tears as she spoke of the suffering that brought a nation to its knees, or that most common of all reminders of war and its continuing effect in peacetime — people with limbs blown away by landmines. And yet, what also was plain to see all around was the sheer determination of the people to make the most of the circumstances they find themselves in — the will to succeed despite the odds.

Putting the past firmly behind them are the dedicated team of teachers, students and musicians, who make up the School of Fine Arts. Here at the school, children from six to eighteen years are given the

opportunity to learn the traditional dances that link them to their ancestors and make up the fabric of their culture. Having been closed during the Khmer Rouge years in power, the school reopened in 1981. A handful of dance teachers who had survived the brutal regime committed themselves to training young dancers, at the same time ensuring an all-round education for the youngsters in their charge. Language instruction is a compulsory part of the curriculum and takes place in the heat of the afternoon, after the students have been taught dance all morning long. From time to time, exceptional dancers are selected to join international dance troupes and their proficiency in foreign languages serves to enhance their career prospects.

I marvelled at the vigour of the morning lessons and the sheer tenacity of these youngsters in striving towards perfection although, admittedly, the discipline involved (sometimes administered with a wooden stick on an offending foot or leg!) made me cringe. As luck would have it, I was invited to stay on for an unusual cultural exchange which was to take place during the late morning. Evidently, it was the reason for the intensity of the earlier gruelling lessons.

What I would never have expected in a million years was about to take place. Dressed to the nines in white tuxedos, a tour busload of middle-aged Korean businessmen filed into the school auditorium, and then sat down. Moments later, the students of the school, the younger children first, began to dance for their visitors. Their programme finished with the school's much-celebrated apsara dancers providing the dance finale. But other entertainment was to come, for at this point the Koreans

Above: After intense rehearsing, this young Khmer dancer is about to perform for foreign visitors. She is unable to conceal her excitement as her friends assist her with her costume.

Opposite: Students practising Khmer dance at the School of Fine Arts in Phnom Penh.

After suffering but surviving the extinctive policies of the Khmer Rouge, Cambodia's rich cultural traditions continue their revival. Here, students are being put through their paces by their teacher.

took the stage and, after thanking the young dancers for their beautiful performance, proceeded to give a full choir recital, complete with piano accompaniment (they had even brought their own piano!). After half a dozen or so Korean songs, their closing numbers included 'Oh Happy Day!' and 'The Hallelujah Chorus', the whole recital clearly appreciated by the audience.

A tour of Phnom Penh would not be complete without visiting the Royal Palace and the famous Silver Pagoda; the glorious terracotta National Museum of Arts with its impressive collection of Khmer art including pre-Angkorian sculptures; and at least some of the many markets. Of the wide range of markets, for fine handwoven silks (old and new) and crafts of Cambodia, the Russian Market offers more, not to mention a colourful array of fruit and Khmer foodstuffs; whereas the Central Market, although the biggest, contains scores of things one would find in certain other markets of Southeast Asian cities — fake labels, dinky electronic gadgetry and the like — all being touted for a song.

Legend has it that the city derived its name from a woman named Penh, who discovered four Buddhas washed ashore on the banks of the Mekong. She kept these holy articles in a monastery she built nearby on a hill. Later, the town that evolved around it became known as Phnom Penh, or the Hill of Penh. Wat Phnom sits on this tree-lined hill, and is a good place from which to view the city. Many locals come to pray before the various stupas, images and shrines, and to make their offerings.

Near Wat Phnom is Phnom Penh's most historic hotel, Le Royal. Much of the film, 'The Killing Fields', is set here. Splendidly renovated by the Raffles Group, Le Royal has reestablished its reputation as one of the finest classic hotels of Southeast Asia. Just a couple of kilometres

Above and above left:
Scenes from one of the
many murals to be
found within the
complex of the Royal
Palace in Phnom Penh.
Opposite: *The Throne*
Hall at the Royal
Palace in Phnom Penh.

Monks walking in the grounds of the Royal Palace in Phnom Penh. The blisteringly hot sun does not deter them from going about their religious duties.

away is the imposing Cambodiana Hotel, spectacularly sited right by the confluence of the Mekong and Tonle Sap rivers.

I told my guide that I wished to go to the Tuol Sleng Museum of Genocide Crime. He said that this would be good for me as it would help me understand better what his people went through. And he was right.

In former times, Tuol Sleng was a high school, complete with playing field. Then, between 1975 and 1978, the Khmer Rouge used the institution as a detention centre, converting classrooms into torture chambers and constructing makeshift concrete-slab walls in larger halls to serve as partitions between prisoners, who then were crammed into tiny cubicles. The grounds were used also, to bury those who did not survive the ordeal. Displayed today are a great many disturbing objects and images. These range from the implements employed in torture to the iron bedstands where the prisoners lay; from the photographs of the victims taken after a session of interrogation to mugshots of every prisoner brought in; from skulls exhumed from the mass grave in the compound to drawings depicting the savagery that took place there. Tuol Sleng serves as a testament of the barbarities perpetrated upon the men, women and children of Cambodia throughout the Khmer Rouge reign of terror. It speaks of the unspeakable, of man's unbelievable inhumanity to his fellow man. Tuol Sleng is no ordinary memorial museum — it leaves the senses numb, casting away much of what one

Above: In Phnom Penh, crossing the road seems as dangerous as walking a tightrope. This woman proves it is all a question of balance.
***Opposite:** Homeward bound! A typical jetty scene on the Tonle Sap River at Phnom Penh.*

might have been expecting to experience here. It is not for those of a weak disposition.

Deciding to visit the nearby river island of Koh Dach, I set off by car, crossing the Mekong on the local cargo ferry. Koh Dach is famous for its exquisite, top-quality handwoven silk and its community of skilful weavers. Almost one in every four houses we passed had a ground-level weaving loom, the centre of activity for the entire household at the weekend, a time when they weren't manning their farms or vegetable patches. Driving through the tranquil island village that it appears today, I found it hard to picture the many armed conflicts that took place here when the village was under siege from the Khmer Rouge.

The long-awaited river journey from Phnom Penh to Siem Reap finally materialized, and along with thirty other travellers I found myself on the deck of a passenger boat, intriguingly named 'Rambo 5', gliding along the Tonle Sap River. Tonle Sap means 'Great Lake', and the river of the same name would lead us to the result of a phenomenon of nature that once supported and sustained an empire.

The Tonle Sap River is one of the great natural wonders of the world. Its fame (and its beneficial effect upon the livelihood of Cambodians) lies in the fact that during several months of the year, it reverses its flow and, as a consequence, regulates the volume of water flowing through the principal river, the Mekong. This reversal occurs during the rainy season, at which time the excess water from the Mekong is safely channelled up the Tonle Sap River and into the Great Lake, which swells anything up to five times its dry-season size. When the rains

Above: *The splendid, French-designed National Museum of Arts in Phnom Penh. The museum contains an interesting collection of Khmer art of which the main focus is on sculpture.*

Opposite: *When you're so young, trying to get the thread of something is a serious business.*

*Above: At a typical
lake-based community
on the Tonle Sap,
these long rolls stored
carefully above the
waterline are bamboo
roofing materials. The
local vegetation provides
a constant supply
of natural building
requisites.*

*Opposite: The Tonle
Sap, or Great Lake,
is a plentiful supplier
of food for the people
who live by its shores.*

have ceased, the lake shrinks as the water flows down into the Mekong again. This incredible phenomenon was once attributed to the Great Kings and still remains cause for celebration and reverence. However, the real reason is that the volume of monsoon water in the Mekong raises the river's level to higher than that of the Great Lake, and so the flow of water in the Tonle Sap River reverses. It comes as no surprise that these rivers serve as lifelines for so many who thrive on the fertile haven created for fish and vegetation on their adjacent plains.

After four hours on the Tonle Sap River, we reached the Tonle Sap itself, the Great Lake. The entire journey had been enthralling, but more so along its final part, where the population becomes more concentrated. The tranquil scenery changes dramatically to floating houses of every description, some beautifully decorated with potted plants and curtains, their dwellers engaged in a host of river-related activities.

We saw fishermen in search of their catch, using every conceivable contraption of net and trap possible — both modern and primitive. We also saw fish being scooped from the lake by hand in the shallows. Floating pigpens became the focus of attention next — their waste is

channelled to provide nourishment for the fish below. As with the whole nation, nothing is wasted, nothing taken for granted in this community.

Approaching Siem Reap, the lake narrows. Here we passed close to the aquatic village settlements of the Vietnamese, Khmer and Cham, and could see their markets, shops and schools as slowly we moved along.

Siem Reap is an unassuming town. Apart from its market, art and craft centre, and a few hotels and restaurants that have sprung up in recent years, it remains relatively quiet and rural. But this may not be so for very much longer, judging by the rising numbers of international tourists visiting the great temples of Angkor. More and more nongovernmental organizations and conservation groups are being concentrated here to assist in restoring the temples and to help the local people adjust to change. For example, training in arts and crafts is seen as a way to provide a livelihood for many, especially those handicapped as a result of landmines or suffering from some other debilitation.

Above and above right: Moving house, literally! Poling a home to a new mooring. And when you move house, your farm moves with you.
Opposite: *Attractive French colonial architecture on Siem Reap's main street.*

The treasures that are to be found nearby are installing Siem Reap firmly on the tourist destination map of the world. Angkor Wat, believed to be the largest religious monument ever built anywhere, and certainly one of the greatest architectural sights the traveller will ever encounter anywhere in the world; the royal city of Angkor Thom, the area within its walls larger than any walled city in mediaeval Europe, even ancient Rome, and containing the Bayon temple-mountain, the Terrace of the Elephants,

the Terrace of the Leper King, the Phimeanakas, and the Baphuon; Bakheng, the temple-mountain to the south of Angkor Thom, from where to view the plain of Angkor; to the east of Angkor Thom, Pre Rup and the haunting, hypnotic Ta Prohm; to the north of Angkor Thom, Preah Khan with Neak Pean and Ta Som close by; and not forgetting Banteay Srei, some 25 kilometres away from Angkor, with its beautiful pink sandstone, vandalized by André Malraux but saved before it was too late; all are part of an endless stream of ancient monuments that entrance and captivate completely. Truly, seeing is believing! I was overwhelmed by the sheer magnificence of Angkor Wat; saddened by the limbless, mutilated statues at Preah Khan; and entirely mesmerized by Ta Prohm in its 'natural' state of fusion and union with the forest. However much time one's schedule allows, it is not enough.

Every temple I visited has its own unique beauty and special story, often recorded in the intricate carvings. My pilgrimage to Angkor was a humbling experience. It made me aware as never before of the huge responsibility we all bear in playing our part to preserve for our children the heritage that is Angkor.

Above: In the Bayon, wherever you turn, wherever you look, you behold 'the smile of Angkor', gazing down at you over 200 times. Whose face and smile? Most experts believe it is that of Jayavarman VII in the form of Avalokiteshvara.

Opposite: The royal city of Angkor Thom is square-shaped. In the centre of each of its four walls is a huge gateway. Shown here is the South Gate.

The nineteenth-century
French explorer, Henri
Mouhot, wrote in the
diary of his travels
that Angkor was more
grand than anything
in Greece or Rome.
The most renowned
of Angkor's monuments
is the breathtaking
Angkor Wat, one of
the great architectural
wonders of the world.

Above: These young girls have just completed performing Khmer classical dance for a group of distinguished visitors at Preah Khan temple.
Opposite: The rambling twelfth-century Preah Khan, was Jayavarman VII's capital before Angkor Thom was completed.

Along the higher reaches of the Mekong, the river plays an integral part in the lives of the people who live near its banks. In Cambodia, playing a part is an understatement — the river is a matter of life and death. Without the waters of this mighty river, and the abundance those waters spawn, particularly in the Great Lake, millions of Cambodians would lose their prime means of self-sufficiency for if, one year, there were to be too little water the harvest would fail. An even greater threat, to people's lives and property, is too much water. Usually, the waters provide a natural balance, and the reputation of the Mekong is of water neither too little nor too much, so much so that Cambodians refer to the river, affectionately, as The Mother of Waters. Nevertheless, the threat of flooding is always there in the background even though such incidences are extremely rare.

Downriver again, immediately after the Tonle Sap River flows into the Mekong at Phnom Penh, the Bassac, the Mekong's major distributary, separates from its parent, and soon takes an almost parallel course with the Mekong, both rivers heading south towards the border with Vietnam. Although the Mekong is now navigable for cargo ships, all the way to the sea, there are no towns of any size between Phnom Penh and the border. The role of the Mekong in Cambodia is at an end and the river soon flows into Vietnam to pursue its deltaic destiny.

*Downriver from
Angkor, back at
Phnom Penh. At
the confluence of the
Tonle Sap and Mekong
rivers, a fishing boat
that would hold its
own at the Great Lake
is positively dwarfed by
a container ship.*

Vietnam

As the Mekong River passes into the final country of its great journey from the Plateau of Tibet to the South China Sea, it opens its jaws to reveal not one mouth but nine (strictly eight, but eight is not a lucky number so a minor outlet is included). The Mekong is now the Cuu Long, meaning Nine Dragons. The Mekong Delta is the name given to this final phase of the river, and it is the main geographical feature of the land south of Ho Chi Minh City.

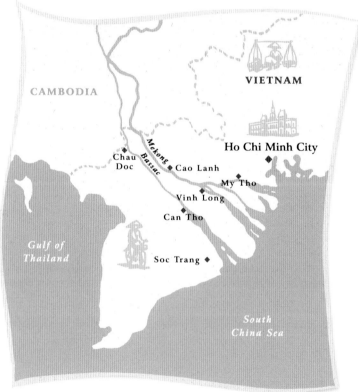

There are no large towns on the Mekong itself as it enters Vietnam, but its distributary, the Bassac River, encounters the city of Chau Doc immediately upon crossing the border. This bustling commercial centre is home to the Hoa Hao religion, whose membership comprises well in excess of a million believers. Essentially, Hoa Hao is a Theravada Buddhist sect but with one major defining difference from the mainstream — it does not believe in temples, maintaining that simplicity of belief is compromised unacceptably by temple worship.

Outside Chau Doc town, the most famous local landmark, the Tay An Pagoda, is highly revered by the Vietnamese. Its most noteworthy features are its huge array of statues, numbering more than 200, and its multiple roofs.

Where once the Mekong, in northwestern China, boasted very few boats, the opposite is true in the Mekong Delta, where ferries taking short, direct routes across the water abound. It is very often the case that

Small cargo boat in the Mekong Delta. Generally, road links in the delta are poor and boats are often the preferred choice.

a road route will take travellers the long way round if, indeed, a road link exists at all.

From Chau Doc, across the Bassac River, then across the Mekong itself, and then downriver is the small town of Cao Lanh. Although rather a sleepy place the countryside around offers magnificent opportunities for viewing birdlife in the delta. Tam Nong Bird Sanctuary is home to around 200 bird species during the year, and My An Bird Garden is remarkable for the tens of thousands of birds that flock together at dawn and dusk, creating vast avian clouds.

The produce harvested here in this area does not go only to the floating markets. Indeed, the bulk goes to Ho Chi Minh City, and from there some is sent to other parts of the country or for export. I particularly wanted to visit Ho Chi Minh City, not only because so many people kept saying I should but also because of that strong commercial connection with the Mekong Delta.

Above and above right: In Ho Chi Minh City, the ubiquitous bamboo pole. With a basket at each end it is a tiny mobile shop.
Opposite: Ho Chi Minh City's markets, teeming with people and with fresh produce.

It was nightfall by the time I arrived in Ho Chi Minh City, or Saigon as it was formerly known until the end of the Vietnam War. The name Saigon still evokes romantic notions of the exotic blend of east and west, a legacy of the period of French colonial influence. Driving through the city, crowded with cars, motorcycles and bicycles, traces of that colonial past live on: spacious boulevards; elegant buildings, particularly many beautiful churches; cafés; baguettes; all serve to remind us of a rich and varied history. When one looks at the city as it is today, it is difficult to

imagine the decades of struggle that her people have had to endure to arrive in the here and now.

For the majority of Vietnamese in Ho Chi Minh City, life is about toil, and toil is a means to an end. The fruits of the labours of the people of the Mekong Delta are very much in evidence on market stalls and in the food stores of Ho Chi Minh City, especially at Ben Thanh, the city's largest market.

An attitude of opportunism makes the city the business hub of Vietnam. It is fully charged with a vibrant energy, whether it be the dynamic style of buying and selling or the purposeful urgency of daily activities. It is little wonder that economic progress and change have come rapidly as the people race full speed ahead.

I spent just a couple of days in Ho Chi Minh City and then began my journey by car towards Can Tho, 150 kilometres south and the largest town on the delta. On the way I would pass through the provinces of Long An, Tien Giang, and Vinh Long, until reaching Can Tho town in the province of the same name.

As I was travelling through the outskirts of Ho Chi Minh City, I stopped to admire an extraordinary and colourful place of worship of the Cao Dai religion. I discovered that Cao Daism is unique to southern Vietnam and has a following of some two million people. Its origins date back to 1919 when Ngo Van Chieu, a civil servant, received a message in a dream. The Cao Dai, or 'Supreme Being', appeared to Ngo in his dream, instructing him to create a new religion by merging the spiritual teachings

Above and above left: *Legacy of the French. City Hall, one of many elegant colonial buildings in Ho Chi Minh City, guarded by an imposing sculpture of Ho Chi Minh.* ***Opposite:*** *Many other colonial buildings are now rather rundown.*

179

Above: A small Cao Dai Temple on the outskirts of Ho Chi Minh City.
Opposite: At the entrance to the Municipal Theatre in Ho Chi Minh City, bandsmen entertain Sunday strollers and cyclists.

of Buddhism, Christianity, Confucianism, Taoism and Islam. It took some time for Cao Dai's instruction to come to official fruition but eventually, in 1926, the religion was launched at a founding ceremony.

The spiritual symbol of Cao Daism is a single, staring, all-seeing, large left eye — left, as it is closer to the heart. This 'Universal Eye' usually appears at the entrance to, and within, Cao Dai churches. Although believers state with simple conviction that Cao Daism serves to unite all other religions, some people hold a different view, claiming Cao Daism was adopted by the people in an attempt to promote a different kind of harmony, namely to help mitigate the effects of the conflicting forces that were tearing Vietnamese society apart during the French period. Perhaps the most intriguing aspect of Cao Daism is its list of saints, a list which includes Moses, Brahma, Joan of Arc, Victor Hugo, William Shakespeare, Sir Winston Churchill, Vladimir Lenin, Sun Yat Sen, and the Vietnamese poet Nguyen Binh Khiem.

After travelling for just 14 kilometres I was in Long An province, famous for the superb quality of its rice. Driving between paddy fields, I was amazed to see stone tombs in the middle of one. Noticing that I was peering quizzically towards them, my driver volunteered that the farmers buried their deceased relatives there for practical reasons. Having them there meant that their graves could be visited easily during workbreaks and thus, by removing the travel factor, loss of precious working time could be avoided. Many observers are convinced that such single-minded dedication to their work contributes to the quality of their crop.

We drove on further, into Tien Giang province. As we neared My Tho, the provincial capital, by the roadside a woman was selling ready-to-eat pineapples, each with the stalk still attached to serve as a handle, and I couldn't resist. Mine tasted deliciously sweet.

My Tho is where, in 1940, worker and peasant organizations involved in local uprisings first raised the red flag emblazoned with a gold star, later to become the flag of North Vietnam and, eventually, the flag of unified Vietnam.

From My Tho I made my way down through the remainder of Tien Giang province, across Vinh Long province, and then waited for the ferry to take me across the Song Hau Giang, one of the mouths of the Mekong. While waiting for the ferry to arrive, a group of women rushed up and crowded round me in an attempt to sell their goods. I was lost in a sea of food. There were baguettes in bamboo baskets, oranges neatly piled up (held in place in a pyramid frame to counteract the jostling), roasted cuu birds (a local speciality) and many other tempting delights.

While I was on the car ferry, I saw workers engaged in the heavy labour of construction. They were building the two-kilometre-long My

Above: Long An students on their way to classes, their uniform the compulsory white ao dai — long tunic, split to the waist each side, and baggy trousers. The ao dai once was mandatory dress for Vietnamese women. Opposite: Life and death in the rice fields. In the midst of emerald fields of life-giving rice, these graves create a surreal portrait in Long An province.

Above: Man selling live birds on the ferry to Vinh Long.
Above right: Delta woman selling cakes.
Opposite: My Thuan Suspension Bridge, viewed from the local ferry. When completed, will the ferry sink into obsolescence, drowned financially by the new bridge?

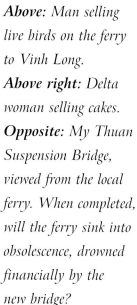

Thuan Suspension Bridge, a project funded jointly by the Vietnamese and Australian governments.

The town of Can Tho is known, unofficially, as the capital of the delta, and is the centre of trade and finance, politics, culture and transportation. Most of the rice grown in the delta is milled here, and the town is home also to a university of the same name, acclaimed for the excellent, ever-popular agricultural courses it offers.

Can Tho is also the main boatbuilding centre of the Mekong Delta, with approximately 60 boatyards. The boats of delta farmers are usually about five metres long, and entirely handmade. It takes only three to four days for just one person to build a boat and so the final price to the farmer is very low. Most farmers find the easiest way to transport their goods is by boat along the canals, especially during the wet season. Unfortunately, the boatbuilders have suffered from a decline in business and several factories have been forced to close down as the demand for boats reduces due to better roads and new and improved bridges serving the delta, whereas until now the river sometimes has been the only option.

I decided to travel on to Soc Trang and then return later to Can Tho. This would be my last side trip and was just three hours away from Can Tho. The town is home to a large Khmer community, and is renowned for its Buddhist temples. Of Cambodian descent, the vast majority of Khmers who live in Vietnam inhabit the Mekong Delta, a region once ruled by Khmer kings. Some Khmers, however, arrived in the delta region relatively recently, escaping from the Pol Pot regime in

Cambodia between 1975 and 1978. Although many returned to Cambodia after the Khmer Rouge were ousted, a significant number have remained in this part of Vietnam.

The Kleang Pagoda in Soc Trang is a fine temple, despite being rebuilt in concrete during 1905 to replace the original bamboo structure of 1533. The temple provides instruction for student monks of the nearby Soc Trang College of Buddhist Education. The Khmer Museum, opposite the pagoda, has an interesting mixture of old and fairly new artifacts, and explains the history and culture of this ethnic minority in Vietnam. It serves as a meeting point and cultural centre, where dance performances are staged from time to time.

Still in Soc Trang I visited the unusual Matoc Pagoda, Maha Tup in Khmer, and also known as the Bat Pagoda. Here, in the trees of the monastery compound, hundreds of these creatures have found a sacred haven wherein to live, completely unthreatened by man. Being in the vicinity of orchards means that they do not have to venture far for food. I found the whole experience of being so close to these nocturnal creatures as they flew all around me an eerie, creepy, uneasy experience. My senses somewhat jarred, I soon beat a hasty retreat, all the way back to Can Tho.

Special features of this part of the Mekong Delta are the floating markets, famed far and wide. Cai Rang, the biggest of the delta, a mere six-kilometre boat ride from Can Tho, is situated on the Can Tho River, a small tributary of the Mekong. Boarding at the unearthly hour of six in the morning proved wise as all market activity was over by nine.

Above and opposite:
The monk is standing outside Kleang Pagoda in Soc Trang. This Khmer temple was originally built of wood, in 1533, and then rebuilt in concrete in 1905.
Above left: *Boats at one of the numerous boatyards in Can Tho.*

Banana boat at Cai Rang floating market in the Mekong Delta.

Above: Local craftware for sale at Phung Hiep's small floating market.
Opposite: Vendors on some boats sell general goods and mixed produce, while some specialize. This boat is large enough to offer several kinds of fruit.

The floating markets in this area are to be found both on the river and on the riverbanks, with many vendors displaying their goods at the top of long upright poles. At Cai Rang, I marvelled at the sight of so many transactions taking place and I watched with interest as all manner of goods were handed over from wholesalers to traders, the latter usually recognizable by the big bamboo baskets hanging on the bows of their boats. Some boats were loaded to the brim with pumpkins, cabbages, carrots or sweet potatoes.

The other two floating markets I visited were at Phong Dien and Phung Hiep. They are a lot smaller than the market at Cai Rang and far less crowded, probably because these markets are primarily for farmers and wholesalers, and it is difficult to purchase anything unless in bulk. In these two markets, although the boats of some vendors are motorized, other vendors stand up in their boats and row around the river.

Can Tho province is well-known for its oranges, guava, pomelo, and dragon fruit (bright pink skin, white flesh dotted with little black seeds) so I went to visit an orchard. Mr. Duong, the proud 'third-generation' owner who inherited it, owns five hectares of orchard land and a plot

reserved for a mausoleum to honour his ancestors. He also grows egg fruit, rarely seen outside Vietnam. Egg fruit has the shape and colour of mango, but tastes like egg yolk.

From Can Tho, it is only 100 kilometres to the Mekong's final destination, the South China Sea. There are no more towns of any size, just small communities. Along the coast, the many mouths of the Dragon pour their waters into the sea, flanked by the lush green delta. Here, the mighty and magical Mekong leaves behind its legacy of rice-filled plains, abundant orchards, and fish harvests rich for the picking. And it leaves behind also the hope that the river will remain kind to those whose lives depend upon its continued beneficence, those very lives it has deigned to touch along its way.

Finally, I have come to the end of my journey down the Mekong. Blessed with good fortune throughout, I have met some of the kindest, most hospitable people ever I could have wished to meet, and discovered life on and around the river as it really is. I have seen hardship, I have seen pride, I have seen the remarkable, I have seen beauty, I have seen joy. Truly, I have seen the magic of the Mekong.

Above: *Coffins for sale! Delivered by boat direct to your door.*
Opposite: *In the delta, garden centres are on the water, not on land!*

At journey's end, my feelings about the Mekong and its people are best summed up in words more eloquent than mine, by Robert Hughes in his poem, 'Mekong River':

Above: *Cai Rang floating market.*
Above right: *Landside, Phung Hiep floating market is full of canvas covers, conical hats, and people, people, people!*
Opposite: *At day's end, this boatman rows his little passenger home.*

So many mouths to feed
where oceans swallow up your flow,
the river's rapid speed
turns into churning, wide and slow.

I ponder where your muddy banks where born,
in frontier China's virgin snow,
and all the harvest tables you adorn;

then think of all of those with cause to mourn,
when months before the harvesttime
the Dragon floods the land and lives are torn.

So many millions forced to climb
into this love-hate paradigm:

hate how you bring on strife,
but love how you bring life.

ACKNOWLEDGEMENTS

I would like to thank the following people whose help during the preparation of 'The Magic of the Mekong' is greatly appreciated:

My sponsor, the Tourism Authority of Thailand, whose support has made publication of this book possible.

Professor Bernard D'Abrera, who inspired and taught me much of what I know about photography, and his wife Lucilla; and Toot Bunnag, a staunch supporter who, with Professor D'Abrera, came up with the idea for the book.

Keith Hardy for his tireless editorial work and invaluable advice throughout; Annie Miniscloux for the design of the book; and Boonyavan Chandraviroj, Ping Amranand and Renu Kurattana for their helpful, professional advice.

My son, Jay, and daughter, Tina, for their substantial input, despite their heavy schedules; my cousin, Arsa Sarasin, and my sister-in-law, Joan Sarasin, for their generous support; and the rest of my family for their encouragement.

Robert Hughes, for permission to use his poem, 'Mekong River', from his collection, 'Beyond Blue Eyes', published by Mark Standen Publishing.

And, finally, Nuanwaln Krairiksh, Marina Samad-Noor and Wandee Arthakor, my intrepid travelling companions at different times, who gave me their time and support.

Julie Sarasin

October 2000

For four decades, the Tourism Authority of Thailand (TAT), a state enterprise of the Royal Thai Government, has provided up-to-date information on various destinations, attractions and activities, and has offered support services covering all aspects of tourism in the Kingdom. Together with the head office, the organization's 22 regional and 15 overseas offices have played an instrumental role in creating a variety of campaigns to market an alluring and desirable product to the global tourism industry.

With the advent of the twenty-first century, and demand by the travelling public for new exciting places, the TAT continues to work tirelessly for the promotion of tourism in Thailand by offering a vast array of attractive choices, making it an internationally favourable destination. This is being enhanced not only by careful planning of sustainable tourism development but also by focusing on the protection and preservation of Thailand's priceless natural and cultural heritage.